INTRODUCTION

This is not so much a study in history, or even in historiography, as in historical causation. Historians and philosophers have written voluminously about the problem of causation in history without clarifying it very much; we present here a case study which is designed to indicate something of the complexity, and something too of the dignity, of the problem.

For though it is not given to us "to know the causes of things," we cannot conclude therefrom that history is chaos, or that it is wholly without meaning, anymore than we can conclude of life itself that it is without meaning, for so to conclude would make thought itself irrelevant. And we must avoid, too, the doctrine of inevitability in history, as we avoid the doctrine of predestination in the ordinary affairs of life, for this doctrine dissipates the sense of public or private responsibility. As the greatest of American historians, Henry Adams, wrote in his autobiography, "As long as he could whisper, he would go on .... begun, bluntly refusing to meet his creator .... mission that creation had taught him nothi..... ....th self respect enough to become effective ....as h...u to ....ount to himself for himself somehow, and to inven. a formula of his own for the universe, if the standard formulas failed."

Certainly there is nothing unusual about this inquiry into the causes of the collapse of the Confederacy. No historian is ever wholly content merely with establishing (in so far as he can establish) *what* happened in history; he must go on and ask *why* it happened. It is this *why* that has fascinated historians from the beginning of time, and that gives excitement and meaning to historical inquiry. Why did Athens flower, in the fifth century B.C., and then suffer defeat in the great Peloponnesian War? Why did the civilization of Carthage disappear almost without a trace? Why did the Roman Empire decline? Why the Renaissance, why the Reformation, why the emergence of nationalism, why the decline of the mighty Spanish empire and the rise to world power of the tiny

5

fog-bound island of Britain, why the American and the French Revolutions? That there are no clear or agreed-on answers to any of these questions does not detract one whit from their interest or their significance.

There is no more illuminating laboratory example of historical causation than the American Civil War. It was fought almost within the memory of living men; and we have an immense body of material designed to record and explain it: probably no other great event is more amply recorded in official records and in the writings of those who participated in it. For the most part attention has been directed to the question of the causes of the war: was it states rights, was it slavery, was it Yankee abolitionists, or Southern fire-eaters, or was it a national neurosis, whatever that is? We direct your attention to a problem equally fascinating and equally puzzling: why did the Confederacy lose the war?

When the Confederacy collapsed, it collapsed all over, and looking back now on that prodigious fall, many of us are inclined to think that it was inevitable from the beginning. As it is inconceivable to most of us that the territory which constitutes the United States should be fragmented into two or twenty nations, it is inconceivable to us that the Confederacy could have made good its bid for independent nationhood. But America south of the Rio Grande is divided into twenty nations, and fragmentation seems to be the rule in nationalism, not consolidation. Certainly the doctrine of the inevitability of Northern victory confronts us with two insuperable difficulties. If it was clear from the beginning that the South must lose, how explain the fact that men like Davis, Benjamin, Rhett, Yancey, Cobb, and scores of others, men who were upright, wise and virtuous, were prepared to lead their section to certain destruction? If defeat was inevitable they must have discerned this, too, and their conduct takes on the character of criminal imbecility. And, second, how explain the general assumption in Europe—and even in parts of the North—that the South would make good her bid for independence? Why were so many otherwise sensible men misled?

It is not too much to say that the South held—or appeared to hold—at least two of the trump cards in 1861. And the reason this appeared to be so is easy to understand. The first trump card was one we would call grand strategy, or ultimate war aims. For the fact is that the Confederacy did not need to win in order to win; it was enough if she held the field long enough to weary the North with the war. The North, in order to win, had to conquer the South—invade and hold an area as great as all western Europe except Italy and Scandinavia—an achievement until then without parallel in modern history. The Confederacy could afford to lose all the battles and all the campaigns, if only she could persuade the North that the price of victory was too high. She asked merely to be left alone, and she proposed to make the war so costly that the North would in the end consent to leave her alone. After all, the American Colonies, and the Netherlands, had achieved independence against even heavier odds.

And this suggests the second trump card that the Confederates held: foreign intervention. The leaders of the Confederacy had read well their history of the American Revolution, or had heard it from their fathers and their grandfathers. They knew that the intervention of France, and then of other European nations, turned the tide in favor of the Americans, and they assumed that history would repeat itself. They counted, therefore, with confidence, on the intervention of Britain and France on their behalf (or on behalf of cotton).

Quite aside from these two major strategic considerations, the South held other advantages. She commanded interior lines, and the ability, therefore, to shift her smaller forces rapidly from one front to another. She was on the defensive, and that position more than made up (so it was thought) for numerical inferiority, since offensive operations, with their requirements of transportation and supply and occupation, demanded a greater superiority than the Union forces could muster.[1] She had

[1] The problem of relative numbers is insoluble, partly because statistics are unavailable, partly because they are unreliable. We can dismiss at once the figures submitted by devout but short-sighted Southerners of 3 million Yankees and only 600,000 boys in gray—figures which are discreditable to the Confederacy because they suggest unwillingness to fight. Frederick Phisterer, statistician of the Union armies, gives a total of 2,772,408 men fur-

a long and deeply indented coastline—one, therefore, which presented almost insuperable difficulties to a blockade. She had, in her three million Negro slaves, a large and on the whole loyal labor force, one which might relieve Southern whites of many civilian duties and permit them to fight. She had, at the beginning, the best generals, and she had a long military tradition.

With all these advantages, why did the South lose? Since 1865 students and historians have pondered this question, without wholly answering it. Curiously enough, the leaders of the Lost Cause had little to say about the reasons for defeat. The greatest of them, Robert E. Lee (there is some reason to suppose that he never expected the Confederacy to win), preserved, after Appomattox, a dignified silence. As Benét says,

> He was the prop and pillar of a State,
> The incarnation of a national dream,
> And when the State fell and the dream dissolved,
> He must have lived with bitterness itself—
> But what his sorrow was, and what his joy,
> And how he felt in the expense of strength,
> And how his heart contained its bitterness,
> He will not tell us.[2]

President Davis wrote two ponderous volumes, but says nothing about the underlying causes of defeat—except

---

nished by or credited to the States and Territories; reducing these to a three-years'-service standard he arrives at a figure of 2,320,272 Union soldiers. Thomas Livermore, whose *Numbers and Losses in the Civil War* is in some ways more reliable, estimates a total Union enlistment of 2,898,304, of whom some 230,000 failed to serve; reducing this figure to a three-year standard he arrives at a total of only 1,556,678 for the Union armies. Estimates of Confederate numbers run from 600,000 to a high of 1,500,000. Livermore's estimate, on a three-year standard, is 1,082,119. Perhaps the closest approximation to the truth is to be found in the census of 1890, which discovered 1,034,073 Union veterans, and 432,000 Confederate veterans still surviving. As life expectancy (and medical services) favored Northerners, these figures suggest roughly a two-to-one ratio for the war itself.

[2] Stephen Vincent Benét, *John Brown's Body* (New York, 1928), Book Four.

to blame his political opponents. Vice-President Stephens, too, produced two unreadable volumes on the Confederacy and the War, but failed to speculate on the question; in his case speculation might have been too embarrassing. Benjamin, the most philosophical mind in the Confederate government, might have given us a really penetrating analysis of the problem, but chose to forget his American past in his English present. Nor do the lesser figures help us much. The literature is voluminous, but curiously unreflective. Perhaps the Southerner of that generation was, as Henry Adams wrote a propos Rooney Lee, unreflective:

> Strictly, the Southerner had no mind; he had temperament. He was not a scholar, he had no intellectual training; he could not analyze an idea, and he could not even conceive of admitting two.

Or—more probably—reflection on the responsibility for so great a catastrophe was simply too uncomfortable. Nor do the Northern participants help us much. Here and there we find a philosophical analysis—in Charles Francis Adams, for example, or in the scientist-philosopher John W. Draper—but by and large Northerners were content with victory or with easy assumptions about the rightness of their cause, the wickedness of the South, or the Providential preference for Union.

But if participants have been strangely silent about this question, historians[3] have been eloquent enough.

[3] It would be tedious to identify or introduce all our historians. Roughly half of them represent the North, half the South; in the actual allotment of space, the South (as might be expected) has a bit the better of it. A few—Charles Francis Adams, Admiral Chadwick, and Colonel Robert Tansill—themselves fought in the war; others—Professor Draper, Rossiter Johnson, James Ford Rhodes, and Edward Pollard—lived through the war and knew many of its leaders. Most of those who speak here are twentieth-century historians, and among them are some who have devoted themselves intensively to the study of the Civil War. Charles Ramsdell, for example, was long regarded as the Dean of Confederate historians as, in all probability, the late Frank Owsley was, too; younger historians like Bell Wiley, Clement Eaton, and Frank Vandiver are their students and disciples. Of the

The trouble is that so few of them are systematic in their eloquence. They speculate, to be sure, but only in connection with the particular inquiry they are conducting or the particular thesis they advance. What emerges from all this speculation is a persuasive demonstration of pluralism in history, or—if you are more cynically minded—of the inability of historians to agree on anything of importance.

Why did the South lose? Was it because the Confederacy was hopelessly outnumbered? But it was, in fact, able to put as many soldiers into action in battle as the Union, until 1864. Was it finances? So a few scholars—among them the learned Ramsdell—have thought, but lack of money did not prevent the Americans from making good their bid for independence. Besides, the financial explanation merely begs the larger question: Why was the Confederacy without money? Was it transportation? The South had a much smaller railroad mileage than the North, but she enjoyed interior lines and had advantages in water communication. Southern transportation facilities were not, in fact, inadequate; the real question is why the South failed to utilize them, or permitted them to disintegrate.

Was it the blockade? But at the beginning of the war the North had only an excuse for a Navy; not until 1863 was the blockade effective. Why did not the Confederacy bring in whatever she needed before that time; why did they not utilize their swift privateers to best advantage? And why were Britain and France ready to respect what was, for a long time, a mere paper blockade? This raises, of course, the vexatious question of foreign intervention. Did the South lose because Britain did not recognize her, did not break the blockade, did not intervene? What was

---

more eminent figures who represent the North, Albert B. Hart was for many years Professor at Harvard University and editor of the American Nation series; Edward Channing, his colleague at Harvard, is remembered for a magisterial six-volume *History of the United States to 1865*; and Allan Nevins, the most prodigiously productive of all American historians, has already brought out four volumes of what promises to be the most comprehensive, scholarly, and critical history of the Civil War period of American history.

wrong with Southern calculations here? Cotton was King and wore a Confederate uniform; why did Britain and France refuse, after all, to acknowledge his power? Was it bad cotton management? Was it bad diplomacy? Was it bad public relations?

Or was the fault, perhaps, in Jefferson Davis, so brittle, so temperamental, so self-assured, so arrogant? He took the conduct of the war into his own hands; he intervened in the military; he had favorites—like the wretched Braxton Bragg—and enmities—as for the brilliant Joseph Johnston; he alienated State governors and Congressmen; he never won the admiration or the affection of the Southern people. Yet on balance Davis emerges as a good President—certainly as good as the Confederacy could have selected at that time: tireless, high-minded, courageous, intelligent, indomitable, right on most major issues far more often than his critics were.

Was the political system of the South to blame, as so many historians persuasively argue? Was the germ of death planted in the Confederacy at birth? Was it possible to create a nation on the basis of states rights, to fight a war, which requires centralization of authority, on the basis of particularism? Well, the United States had been created on that basis—at least so Southerners thought (and so the Articles of Confederation asserted)—and had managed to win independence nonetheless.

Was it perhaps slavery that was the cause not only of the war, but of Southern defeat? There is a seductive poetic appeal about such an explanation. Perhaps slavery was the Achilles' heel of the South; slavery prevented foreign recognition; slavery gave the North a new goal and a new ideal; slavery encouraged states rights; slavery in the end weakened the economy and the military effort more than it strengthened them.

Or perhaps it was all of these things combined—something which, for want of a better term, historians call "loss of nerve." The fall of Rome has been ascribed to that mysterious thing called "loss of nerve," and so too, in our own time, the decline of the West. Did the South, in the end, lose its nerve? Perhaps so, but we still want to know why the mettlesome South of 1861 became the nerveless South of 1865. To argue that defeatism causes defeat is a circular argument that gets us nowhere.

Two things should be clear to anyone who considers these interpretations: first that the defeat of the Confederacy was not inevitable, and second, that causation is not simple but complex, not singular but plural. And the student will do well to reflect that the failure of the Confederacy to achieve independence is not a unique miscalculation in history: the whole of history is bestrewn with mighty miscalculations. On almost every page we see written the words of Euripides:

> The end men looked for cometh not,
> And a path there was, where no man thought;
>   So hath it fallen here.

Part I

SOUTHERN ADVANTAGES

1. Charles Francis Adams: ALL THE IMPARTIAL OBSERVERS EXPECTED THE SOUTH TO WIN *

At the close of his summary of the war, in that chapter devoted to a consideration of the internal affairs of the Confederacy during the struggle, Mr. (James Ford) Rhodes suggests a query which I have often put to myself, and over which I have, first and last, pondered much. Tersely stated, it is this:—How was it that we ever succeeded in overcoming the seceded States? . . .

The usual and altogether conventional explanation given is the immense preponderance of strength and resources—men and material—enjoyed by one of the two contending parties. The census and the statistics of the War Department are then appealed to, and figures are arrayed setting forth the relative population and wealth, —the resources, manufactures and fighting strength of the two sides. As the result of such a showing, a certain amount of astonishment is finally expressed that the Confederacy ever challenged a conflict; and the conclusion reached is that, under all the circumstances, the only real cause for wonder is that such an unequal contest was so long sustained.

But this answer to the question will hardly bear examination. After the event it looks well,—has a plausible aspect; but in 1861 a census had just been taken, and every fact and figure now open to study was then patent. The South knew them, Europe knew them; and yet in the spring of 1861, and from Bull Run in July of that year to Gettysburg and Vicksburg in 1863, no unprejudiced observer anywhere believed that the subjugation

* Charles Francis Adams, "Mr. Rhodes's Fifth Volume," *Proceedings, Massachusetts Historical Society*, 2nd series, Vol. XIX (1905), pp. 315-316.

of the Confederacy and the restoration of the old Union were reasonably probable, or, indeed, humanly speaking, a possibility. Mr. Gladstone, a man wise in his generation, and as a contemporaneous observer not unfriendly to the Union side, only expressed the commonly received and apparently justified opinion of all unprejudiced on-lookers, when at Newcastle, in October, 1862, he made his famous declaration in public speech that "Jefferson Davis and other leaders of the South . . . have made a nation. . . . We may anticipate with certainty the success of the Southern States so far as regards their separation from the North. I cannot but believe that that event is as certain as any event yet future and contingent can be." No community, it was argued, numbering eight millions, as homogeneous, organized and combative as the South, inhabiting a region of the character of the Confederacy, ever yet had been overcome in a civil war; and there was no sufficient reason for supposing that the present case would prove an exception to a hitherto universal rule. All this, moreover, was so. Wherefore, then, the exception? How was it that, in the result of our civil war, human experience went for nothing? . . .

2. Albert Bushnell Hart: SOUTHERN ADVANTAGES IN GEOGRAPHY *

At the beginning of the struggle, the advantage of geographical situation seemed to be decidedly with the South. Leaving out of account the Territories and the two States of the Pacific Slope, which entered very little into the military contest, the remaining seventeen free States had, in 1860, 768,255 square miles, while the fifteen slave-holding States had an area of 875,743 square miles. . . .

Inferior as the South was in its products, it was strong in natural defenses. The Atlantic and Gulf coasts abounded in shallow harbors not easily penetrable by a hostile force. It was a coast difficult to invade, yet fur-

* Albert Bushnell Hart, "Why the South Was Defeated in the Civil War," *Practical Essays on American Government* (New York, 1893), pp. 263-268.

nishing many havens from which cruisers and privateers might sally forth. Throughout the war no progress was made by Northern armies moving inward from the seaboard, except on the Mississippi.

From the valley of the Shenandoah to northern Alabama the South was flanked by a natural and impregnable defense, the Appalachian chain of mountains. In the conditions of military transportation at that time it was impossible for a large army to carry with it the supplies for men and animals necessary for a march of a hundred miles through a mountain region. At the beginning of the war Lincoln, with the supreme commonsense which, when applied to military matters, made him often a better general than the generals, suggested that a railroad should be built southeast from some point on the Ohio River, to penetrate the mountain system. The next few years showed that had that counsel been followed it might have shortened the war, by a year; for the only country between Harper's Ferry and northern Mississippi which at that time was penetrated by a railroad leading from north to south was the rugged region lying between Chattanooga and Atlanta. Down that line of railroad Sherman fought his way in 1864; and from Atlanta he proceeded on the march which cut the Confederacy in twain. Except upon that line of railroad the South proved impregnable to land assault from the northwest.

Another vast geographical advantage which the South possessed at the beginning of the war disappeared in 1863. By its control of the mouth of the Mississippi, the Southern Confederacy expected to compel the friendship, if not the adhesion, of the upper Mississippi States. The South believed that it held in its hand the key to the commerce of the interior of the Union, and an early act of the Confederate Congress declared the Mississippi open to the friends of the Confederacy. But the Erie Canal and the four lines of trans-Alleghany railways, the New York Central, Erie, Pennsylvania Central, and Baltimore & Ohio, united the West still more strongly to the East. The Northwestern States saw, aside from all moral questions connected with slavery, that the success of the Union meant that both the eastern and the southern highways would be opened, while the success of the

Confederacy meant that one or the other must be in the hands of a hostile power. Whatever the expectations of the South, the capture of New Orleans in 1862, and of Vicksburg, July 4, 1863, not only dismembered the Confederacy, but quieted the fears of the northern interior States. Thenceforward, as Lincoln wrote, "the Father of Waters rolled unvexed to the sea."

Another military advantage for the South was the sparseness of its population, and the fact that a great part of the theatre of war was untilled. Except in the Shenandoah Valley, to a less degree in Mississippi, the Federal armies could nowhere support themselves from the country until Sherman's march to the sea in 1864. They advanced through regions heavily wooded, and they advanced into an enemy's country. The South had not only the advantages of situation, but of fighting in the midst of a friendly population and fighting on the inside lines. However unpractical the transportation system of the South, it was much easier to move troops from Richmond to Atlanta than from Washington to the Mississippi. In a word, the theatre of the war was finally narrowed to the strip of territory between the western edge of the mountains and the sea. Within that strip a smaller number of troops could make head against a larger number; and in the later stages of the war two hundred thousand Confederate troops kept a million Northern soldiers employed. . . .

Part II

THE TRADITIONAL VIEW: OVERWHELMING FORCE

3. John William Jones: THE OVERWHELMING POWER OF THE NORTH *

If called upon to give in a single sentence the cause of the failure of the Confederates to succeed in their great struggle for constitutional freedom, I would quote from General Lee's valedictory address to the remnant of his army at Appomattox. He says:

> After four years of arduous service, marked by unsurpassed courage and fortitude, the army of northern Virginia has been compelled to yield to overwhelming numbers and resources. I need not tell the brave survivors of so many hard-fought battles, who have remained steadfast to the last, that I have consented to this result from no distrust of them, but feeling that valor and devotion could accomplish nothing that would compensate for the loss that would have attended the continuance of the contest, I determined to avoid the useless sacrifice of those whose past services have endeared them to their countrymen.

This sentence of the great chieftain might be applied to all of the armies of the Confederacy, and to the Confederate government. They made a struggle which astonished the world, and gained victories which illustrated brightest pages of the annals of history, but were finally "obliged to yield to overwhelming numbers and resources."

We know not how better to state the comparative preparation of each section for the war than to quote from an article of Benjamin J. Williams, Esq., of Massa-

---

* John William Jones, "Why the Southern Confederacy Failed," *The South in the Building of the Nation*, Vol. IV (Richmond, Va., 1909-1913), pp. 544-546.

chusetts, published in the Lowell *Sun* some years after
the war:

> The odds in numbers and means in favor of the North
> were tremendous. Her white population of nearly 20,000,000
> was fourfold that of the strictly Confederate territory;
> and from the border Southern states and communities of
> Missouri, Kentucky, East Tennessee, West Virginia, Mary-
> land and Delaware, she got more men and supplies for
> her armies than the Confederacy got for hers. Kentucky
> alone furnished as many men to the Northern armies as
> Massachusetts. In available money and credit the advantage
> of the North was vastly greater than in population, as it
> included all the chief centres of banking and commerce.
> Then she had possession of the old government, its capital,
> its army and navy, and mostly its arsenals, dock-yards and
> workshops, with all their supplies of arms and ordnance,
> and military and naval stores of every kind and the means
> of manufacturing the same. Again, the North, as a manu-
> facturing and mechanical people, abounded in factories
> and workshops of every kind, immediately available for
> the manufacture of every kind of supplies for the army and
> navy, while the south, as an agricultural people, were
> almost entirely wanting in such resources. Finally, in the
> possession of the recognized government, the North was in
> full and free communication with all nations, and had full
> opportunity, which she improved to the utmost, to import
> and bring in from abroad not only supplies of all kinds,
> but men as well for her service, while the South, without
> a recognized government, and with her ports speedily
> blockaded by the Federal navy, was almost entirely shut
> up within herself and her own limited resources.

Unquestioned official figures show that the Federal
government enlisted during the war 2,326,168 men, while
the Confederacy enlisted only 600,000, making the Federal numerical superiority 1,726,168.

The United States army was made up, in part, of
Germans, 176,800; Irish, 144,200; British-Americans,
53,500; English, 45,500; other foreigners, 74,900; Negroes, 186,017; total, 680,917; or an excess of 80,917
of the total enlistment in Confederate armies.

There were Southern men in the Federal armies, including those from Maryland, Kentucky and Missouri,
316,424. Adding to these the foreigners and negroes, and
they make 997,341, or 397,341 more men than were enlisted in the Confederate armies.

There were in the Federal armies of soldiers enlisted from Northern states 1,325,297, or more than twice as many as the enlistments in the Confederate armies. Is it any wonder that with such "overwhelming numbers and resources" against them that the Confederacy was at last forced to yield? . . .

4. Rossiter Johnson: THE ABSURDITY OF THE SOUTHERN ATTEMPT TO FIGHT *

When the Southern people entered upon the attempt at secession, they committed themselves to four capital absurdities: First, they went out with ten millions to meet those who could come against them with twenty millions. Second, they proposed to divide a great country along a line where there was no natural barrier—a line, moreover, that was crossed by great arteries of commerce. Third, they attempted to reverse the economical and political tendencies of a thousand years and divide instead of uniting. Fourth, to save an institution from gradual destruction they undertook a task that, if accomplished, would only have accelerated its decay.

With these facts and principles in mind, it seems natural and reasonable to say that such a war as the insurrection of 1861 could not have any turning points, for it would be a foredoomed failure. In the long view this is probably correct; and one of the ablest of the Southern military leaders, perhaps the very ablest, has since expressed the opinion that if separation had been effected the sections ultimately would have come together again. Yet there were other circumstances which gave the bloody enterprise a chance of immediate if not permanent success, and the apparent turning points—the events that shaped and prolonged the contest—are quite discoverable.

Of the four absurdities or insoluble problems that I have pointed out, the Southern people appeared to take recognizance of but one—the discrepancy in wealth and population—and this they disposed of to the satisfaction

* Rossiter Johnson, "Turning Points in the Civil War," *Annual Report, American Historical Association* (1894), pp. 41-44.

of their own minds by three reliances: First, their own superior prowess. They professed to believe, and probably most of them did believe, that, as material for an army, they were altogether superior to the men of the North; that everyone of them would be equal to three or four of the enemy, just as one white soldier is equal to three Indians in a fight on our Western frontier. There was a grain of truth in this, for nearly every man in the South had learned to ride and shoot, while in the North comparatively few had those accomplishments, and at the outset this discrepancy was apparent, but it soon wore away. Second, they counted upon assistance from a political party in the North, and here, too, their expectation seemed not altogether unreasonable, for some of the leaders of that party—notably one who had been President, and one who afterward was a candidate for that office—assured the insurgents, in the strongest terms, of the sympathy and active assistance of their party. But in these declarations Mr. Pierce and Mr. Seymour, as the event proved, committed themselves to an absurdity. It might be true that the Northern wing of their party would grant everything to the Southern wing so long as it remained in the Union, but to help it to get out of the Union, leaving the Northern Democrats in a hopeless minority, would be to commit suicide. The Democratic party of the North did not directly do any such thing— although it did some things that tended indirectly toward that end, and undoubtedly prolonged the war—and many of the most skillful and devoted soldiers in the National Army were Democrats. Third, they believed that as the Southern States were the great producers of cotton, Great Britain would not long allow their ports to be closed and her looms to be kept idle. This, too, seemed a fair reliance, and yet it utterly failed them, for a reason that requires too much explanation to be entered upon here. As France had assisted the thirteen colonies to throw off their allegiance to England, our Southern citizens found it easy to believe that England in turn would help them to their independence, and the successful result of the Revolution of 1776 was constantly cited as proof that the Southern States could not be conquered even by such superiority in resources and men as the North possessed. The undistributed middle is to be found in the difference between the Atlantic Ocean and Mason and Dixon's line.

While the mass of the Southern people ignored all but the first of the four problems, it seems probable that their leaders recognized the importance of at least one of the others—that relating to a natural boundary. The Potomac and the Ohio would have afforded something like a natural boundary, though an imperfect one, and in the formation of the Confederacy the greatest anxiety to include the border States was shown. A record of this is to be found in the Confederate constitution, where it was provided that the Confederate Congress might at anytime pass a law forbidding importation of slaves into the Confederacy from any State or Territory that was not a member of it. This was a threat at the slave breeding industry of Virginia and Kentucky; and there is reason to believe that it had a powerful influence in dragging Virginia out of the Union. So anxious were the secession leaders to secure these States that when the Virginia convention passed a provisional ordinance of secession, which was not to become operative unless a majority of the people of the State voted in favor of it, the capital of the Confederacy was removed at once from Montgomery, Ala., to Richmond, Va., weeks before the day appointed for the people of the State to elect whether they would leave the Union. I believe history does not furnish another instance of a government officially establishing its capital on foreign soil.

But while Virginia, as Farragut expressed it, was "dragooned out of the Union," Kentucky refused to go out on any consideration, although many of her citizens were secessionists. And that refusal was the first turning-point in the great struggle.

With Kentucky as a part of the new Confederacy, the natural line of defense west of the Alleghanies would have been along the Ohio River. But when Kentucky nominally declared herself neutral and practically remained true to the Union, thousands of her sons taking service in its armies, the line of defense was pushed back to her southern border, where there is no natural barrier. The Confederates attempted to establish an artificial defensive line running through Mill Spring, Bowling Green, and Columbus, with Forts Henry and Donelson at the points where it crossed the Tennessee and Cumberland rivers. Against an equipped and determined enemy it is impossible to hold such a line. In January, 1862, this one was broken through by a force under Col. James A. Garfield, which moved up Big Sandy River and defeated the force under Humphrey Marshall at Paintville; by Gen. George H. Thomas, nine days later, at Mill Spring, where he defeated the Confederates under General Zollicoffer; and by General Grant in February, when he captured Forts Henry and Donelson and swept away the last remnant of the line. Grant's brilliant victory at Donelson, where he demanded unconditional surrender and captured 14,000 men, gave the Unionists the first real inspiration of military ardor and martial pride. It was now plainly evident to those who comprehended the military situation that the "back door of the Confederacy," as it was called, stood open, though in fact, through Kentucky's refusal, it never had been closed. The army of Grant went southward, following the course of the Tennessee River, fought and won the battle of Shiloh (or Pittsburg Landing) in April, and later captured Corinth. There was no reason then why it should not have proceeded to the Gulf or into the heart of the Confederacy, and it was certain that ultimately it would, though timid counsels at Washington delayed the movement two years. . . .

Part III

A GENERAL SURVEY OF
THE CAUSES OF DEFEAT

5. Colonel Robert Tansill: WHY THE SOUTH LOST: A POTPOURRI OF CAUSES *

Beginning of Secession—Sentiments of the People

The Southern people were involved from the very commencement of the contest in those unfortunate embarrassments which always invite and precede a fall. The tardiness with which some of the States seceded, others not at all, and the divisions among the people in regard to secession, inspired the United States Government with the hope and belief that they would offer but a feeble resistance. This, doubtless, more than anything else, induced the North to prosecute the war. Such were the state of affairs in the South when President Lincoln issued his Proclamation, calling for seventy-five thousand troops. This Proclamation produced great excitement and indignation among the people, and decided them at once in favor of secession. All classes were animated with great zeal and enthusiasm in their cause. No people were then ever more united. It was indeed a sublime spectacle, to behold a brave and generous people arming and rushing to the field in defence of their menaced liberty, and all that honorable men hold dearest upon earth. And had their heroic bravery, generous sacrifices, and noble patriotism been directed by a wise and just policy, a competent and magnanimous government, they would have come out of the struggle triumphant. But it was for some wise purpose decreed otherwise. And although defeat has made "all their sacred things profane," still they have

* Colonel Robert Tansill, *Free and impartial exposition of the causes which led to the failure of the Confederate States to establish their independence* (Washington, 1865), pp. 5-13.

23

preserved their honor as an inheritance for their posterity. This indeed is a glorious and priceless legacy, and is all— all they have preserved from the mighty wreck. But, by manly and Christian-like patience under long suffering, they will ultimately regain more than they have lost. All the ills of this life are only blessings in disguise.

I proceed to notice what I regard as the principal causes which led to the failure of the Confederate States to maintain their Independence.

I. They committed a great mistake in not seceding before the 4th of March, 1861. Had all the States seceded before that period, formed a government, and organized a strong and well-disciplined army, with good officers, which they could readily have done, it is more than probable that the war and its terrible consequences would have been averted, and the Independence of the Confederacy established without shedding a drop of blood. But be this as it may, had the South been thus prepared for the contest, it is certain that the war would have had a different termination, and the Southern people spared the great and almost unparalleled misfortunes and humiliations to which they have been subjected.

II. Foreign Recognition and Aid

Both the Confederate Government and people placed too much reliance upon foreign recognition and succors instead of relying entirely upon their own resources, and making preparations commensurate with the great interests involved, and the magnitude of the war when hostilities first commenced. This was a great error, and injuriously affected their cause throughout the whole period of the war. They ought to have known that, while monarchical governments would be lavish in expressions of sympathy for their cause, because it was weakest and as a matter of courtesy, yet they could not but be averse to the principles for which they were contending, inasmuch as they struck at the very foundation of their own governments, and view with inward satisfaction convulsions which tended every moment to strengthen and cement their own system of government and authority. The foreign policy of these governments is directed more by ambition, selfishness and revenge, than any love they have for liberty or justice. Those who deny this know but little of mankind.

France did not assist our forefathers in their struggle for independence for love of justice or liberty. Not at all. Her aid was given in order to humble the pride and reduce the power of Great Britain, her great maritime rival, and an ardent desire to recover the losses which she had recently sustained, and to restore the glory of her arms, (so dear to Frenchmen,) which had been tarnished by defeats in her late war with England. What interest or motives could England have to interpose in the internal quarrels of a people who had caused her such humiliation, and cost her so much blood and treasure, and torn from her crown its fairest jewels.

Had England joined France in her proposed overtures of peace to the belligerents, and a war with the United States had grown out of them, which was more than likely, it would, in all probability, in the ever changing feelings and interests of nations, have terminated in an alliance between France and the United States, by which France, with the aid of steam and her great military power, might have thrown three or four hundred thousand troops into England to efface the unpleasant recollections of Waterloo and St. Helena, and some French marshal might now be enjoying the distinguished honor of having conquered the great British Empire. Such things were by no means impossible. But the English government is conducted by statesmen, and not politicians, who, well knowing that alliances and compacts, however just or solemn, offer but a slender bar to cupidity and ambition, and that there is but a single day between an alliance and war, wisely determined to avoid all such contingencies by abstaining from all interference in a contest in which she had all to lose and nothing to gain.

France, however, could have recognized the Confederate States and aided them with her arms, without the slightest danger to her national existence, and thereby have acquired great commercial advantages. But both of these nations preferred to permit the parties at war to continue to prolong the struggle until they exhausted themselves, and by the manner in which it was prosecuted to destroy the charm of Republics in the eyes of the world, in which they have too well succeeded.

Governments, like all corporations, have no souls, and, as I have before observed, are, in their conduct towards other nations, controlled by the cold principle of selfishness and ambition; which fact the history of the world fully demonstrates.

III. Currency

Early in the first year of the war Congress created a paper currency without imposing taxes to prevent its depreciation, nor were any assessed, proportionate to the expenses of the war, until 1863. The enormous amount of paper money issued by the Government, from 1861 to 1863, without levying taxes commensurate with its expenditures, caused, as was natural, a rapid depreciation in the currency. So great had been the depreciation that, in the month of December, 1862, one dollar in gold would bring eight dollars in paper; December, 1863, one dollar in gold would buy eighteen dollars in paper; December, 1864, one dollar in gold was worth thirty-four dollars in paper; February, 1865, one dollar in gold commanded sixty-five dollars in paper; and, after the surrender of General Lee's army in April, one dollar in gold was worth from five hundred to one thousand dollars in paper, which was next to worthless.

When it is remembered that money is one of the principal sinews of war, it seems strange that the Government did not adopt timely measures to sustain its credit, whereas the failure to do so had a considerable share in its destruction. They unwisely assumed that "Cotton was King," and proposed to make this King coerce Foreign Intervention. Fatal error! If they had only justly measured the proportions of the coming struggle, and had placed their cotton in England to the credit of the Confederate Government—enthroned there, he would have been King indeed. It would have been the magic source of a stream of gold that would have banished even the apprehension of want from the land, and formed the basis of a financial system that would have maintained the credit of the Government at home and abroad. Verily Cotton would have been King of Might, if he had been crowned in the right place.

As all who assisted by their conduct in bringing about a catastrophe which has caused so much misery and humiliation, should bear their just share, it is but proper to observe that Congress passed a law providing for the reduction of the currency in circulation by funding it in Confederate bonds; but the people were seized with such a mania for money-making, that they desired more to use the funds in speculations than invest them in these bonds; thus preferring their private interests to the public good, by which they lost all; a melancholy evidence of the inconsistency and weakness of poor human nature. And although such obliquity of judgment does not detract from the merit or grandeur of the cause itself, yet it cannot but inspire the most painful regret.

But in all wars, no matter how just or sacred the cause, there will be found individuals who prefer their personal interest to their duty, and the profitable to the honest.

IV. Conscription Law—Its Pernicious Effects

Nearly all the Confederate Army having been unwisely enlisted but for one year, the most of the soldiers' term of service would expire in the spring of 1862; and, as but a few would voluntarily re-enlist, Congress found it necessary to pass a conscription law in the winter of that year to prevent the dissolution of the army, thus at once bringing about the ruin of their cause.

Although this law was required and justified by the public good, it contained a provision permitting the soldiers to furnish substitutes, which was both impolitic and unjust, and had, as ought to have been anticipated, a pernicious effect upon the army, as it enabled all those who could raise sufficient funds to purchase substitutes to escape the hardships and dangers of the field, and those who were unable to do so had, of course, to remain in the army.

V. Short Enlistments—Evil Effects Thereof

It was a capital oversight in the Confederate and State Governments in failing to enlist their troops for the whole period of the war, when it first commenced; for, as is usual at the beginning of all political revolutions, great unanimity and patriotic zeal prevailed amongst the people throughout the country, which rendered that measure both feasible and easy. But lost opportunities seldom return, and are often fatal, especially in war. This important measure, so easy at the outset of the war, was quite impossible in its advanced stages, as the ardor of the people is always cooled or abated by the hardships and vicissitudes inseparable from a state of hostility. This fact suggests painful reflections, one of which is, that although the advantages and blessings of freedom are so numerous and precious, no people have yet successfully maintained it without first establishing a despotism for themselves.

VI. Military Elections Detrimental to Discipline

Congress, with the view of rendering the conscription law as acceptable as possible to the army, inserted a clause in that act authorizing the companies to elect their officers, and the company officers to elect the field officers, a policy subversive of good order, military discipline, and efficiency. Thus one wrong nearly always induces another. By these elections many officers of real merit, who had served with honor and distinction, were lost to the army, and their places filled, with few exceptions, by incompetent ones, which seriously impaired the strength and efficiency of the army, from which it never entirely recovered, and is one of the many influences which led to its final overthrow. Not a few of the newly elected officers could either command respect or obedience, consequently, as is usual in all armies not restrained by rigid discipline, the soldiers abandoned themselves to their disreputable propensity for pillage, which was carried to such a disgraceful extent as to become a disastrous scourge upon the citizens whom they were formed to protect. These outrages unfortunately tended to abate, to some extent, the devotion of the people for a cause so just, and which they loved so well. These disorders also weakened the attachment of the citizens for the Government to whom they are ever willing to impute their misfortunes, even when brought on by themselves.

Military history clearly proves that an army to be equal to a prolonged contest, must be under severe discipline and competent officers, without which it is incapable of any great enterprise, and must, in the end, be vanquished.

The many evils and dangers experienced during our war of Independence with England, from military elections and short enlistments, which brought the Colonists several times to the brink of ruin, and from which they were only saved at last by the assistance of the French, should, it would seem, have warned the Government from adopting a policy ever fraught with so many difficulties and dangers. But neither nations or individuals learn much from experience. If they did, the world would not so often be afflicted with that most terrible of all calamities—war.

VII. Slavery

Although Slavery was physically an element of strength to the South, yet it had, morally, a prejudicial influence upon her cause.

A very large portion of the world affected or found it convenient to condemn an institution which they had been entirely instrumental in introducing into the South, and refused to recognize or succor a people in their heroic struggle for freedom who deserved their admiration and cordial support.

VIII. Political Dissensions

As I have already remarked, the war commenced with remarkable unity and fervor, among all classes of the people. Still old political feuds and animosities lurked in the bosoms of many, only waiting for an opportunity for development. Even as early as the second year of the war, as its hardships began to be more sensibly felt, and success not appearing so certain, a factious spirit was manifested towards the Government in different parts of the country, particularly in North Carolina and Georgia. The ardor of the people was already greatly abated, and President Davis had lost much of his popularity.

In all political convulsions there are always to be found individuals, who, governed by ambition, self-interest, and revenge, prove faithless to their cause. The Confederacy experienced no little detriment and embarrassment through such defection, and it is indeed the chief cause of its final ruin. This faction originated in the belief that the South would fail, and its members determined to seek their own advantage by accelerating its fall. They did everything in their power to discourage the citizens, and to bring defeat upon the Confederate arms. Its increase in numbers and boldness was in proportion to the misfortunes of the country—a melancholy example of human depravity.

In 1863-'4, this party had so increased by desertions from the army and accessions from the citizens, that it was really formidable. In North Carolina, they adopted the name of "Conservatives," which meant destruction, as their subsequent conduct too well attests. They denounced the Confederacy as a despotism, and proclaimed in their newspapers that it was a "rich man's war and a poor man's fight." They were actuated by no other motive than the destruction of the country for their own benefit, and many of these men had been the most zealous advocates of secession. Thus it is seen that the most ultra professors of devotion to a cause, are not always the most constant in their opinions and conduct.

Liberty is never so much endangered as by the disputations of unprincipled and ambitious politicians. "They were not born for their country, but themselves."

But the retribution of Providence is certain, and it sometimes falls upon the guilty even in this world. No man should be blamed for his opinions, for he cannot help them. We can only deal with facts. But no man should espouse a cause that he does not believe right and just, and when he does, he should prove faithful to the last. But enough. To me this is a disagreeable subject. I have referred to it with reluctance—I dismiss it with impatience. . . .

Part IV

THE FAILURE OF LEADERSHIP

6. John W. Draper: THE BLINDNESS OF SOUTHERN LEADERS *

In the opinion of the Adjutant General . . . the available Confederate force capable of active service in the field did not, during the entire war, exceed 600,000 men. Of this number not more than 400,000 were enrolled at any one time, and the Confederate States never had in the field more than 200,000 men capable of bearing arms.

He believes that one third of all the men actively engaged on the Confederate side were either killed outright upon the field, or died of disease and wounds; another third were captured, and held for an indefinite period in Northern prisons; and of the remaining third, at least one half were lost to the service by discharges and desertion. At the close of the war the available force of the Confederate States numbered scarcely 100,000 effective men, and this number he declares was all that was opposed to one million of Federal troops. Such are the Confederate estimates.

If these statements are to be accepted, the conduct of those who directed the war in behalf of the Confederacy is without justification. So long as it was believed that the secession movement might be ventured upon without provoking hostilities, its promoters may present an excuse, but not so after the great disparity of the contending forces became a demonstrated fact. There is a point beyond which no commander has a right to risk his men— the point at which it has become clear that it is physically impossible for them to attain his object. Already the South is justly asking, Who is it that shall bear responsibility for what has happened? who is it that has ruined us? It is no answer to this question to say that "the resolu-

* John W. Draper, *History of the American Civil War*, Vol. III (New York: Harper & Brothers, 1870), pp. 651-654.

tion, unsurpassed bravery, and skill with which the Confederate leaders conducted this contest is shown by the fact that, out of 600,000 men in the field, about 500,000 were lost to the service;" it is of no use to boast that the South maintained her ground for a time against a force ten times as strong as her own. She can not accept a compliment to her animal courage at the expense of her common sense.

Who was it that ruined the South? Incompetent political leaders, an unfaithful clergy, a profligate press.

What but ruin could be the result when the political leaders were deceiving their constituents as to the intentions, the temper, the power of the adversary they were provoking; when the clergy were justifying, as an ordinance of God, the darkest crime of the age; when the press was goading the people to the perpetration of civil war, and, that accomplished, persistently misrepresenting its events from the beginning to the end.

Incompetent political leaders! No one can study the acts of the Richmond administration without being struck with the shortcomings of Davis as a ruler. It was impossible that, under such guidance, there could be success. The people gave him whatever he asked for without deduction or delay—their men, their wealth, all that they had were his. Yet, no matter in what direction we look, whether in the military, the diplomatic, the legislative, the financial, we recognize nothing but failure. Not a trace of genius in any of these departments is to be seen. The war was alternately carried on with brute energy and vacillation, with explosions of passion and tricks of intrigue, but never with deliberate skill. The best officers in the army were put down to make way for favorites; the deep-seated convictions and earnest entreaties of an agonized people were set at naught. The means lavishly given to secure independence were squandered, not used. There is scarcely one of the public addresses of Davis which does not surprise us with its indiscretion, its intemperance, or shock us with its ferocious vulgarity. Long before the close of the war it became obvious to the ablest men in the Confederacy, to those who were in a position to judge correctly of the state of affairs, that success, under such leadership, was impossible. How could it be otherwise? History, as yet, offers no exception to the declaration of Tacitus: "No man ever administered well an empire won by crime."

In the movement undertaken by the South there was an incompatibility between the political and the military conditions. The highest statesmanship was necessary to reconcile them, yet reconciled they must be if success was to be obtained. The military condition required heavy taxation, the political opposed it; the political required Northern invasion, the military forbade it; the military required the use of the slave as a soldier, the political dared not yield him; the military required foreign aid, French armies and English fleets, the political would not give the purchase-consideration that was needful to secure them—Emancipation. State rights must be reconciled with the wrongs of Confederate conscription; the abandonment of important regions to the ravages of the enemy, with the constitutional obligation to defend them. In face of the imbecility with which public affairs were transacted —an imbecility unconcealable even from the men in the ranks—the conscript, taken by force, perhaps carried in chains, unpaid for his services, his family left in starvation at home, was to be transmuted into an enthusiastic soldier. Need it be wondered at that before the close of the war two thirds of the Confederate army had deserted? How could there be enthusiasm when there was no faith? Faith in the head of the Confederacy was gone.

Iron quickly receives the excitement of magnetism, and as quickly loses it. Steel receives it reluctantly, but retains it permanently. In its military enthusiasm the South exhibited a rapid decline. They who clamored for war in the beginning were on the roll of deserters in the end. The South had the magnetism of soft iron, the North that of tempered steel. The energies of the latter, excited by the outrage of Sumter and the defeat at Bull Run, went on increasing, and were very far from having reached their maximum at the close of the war.

The decline of the military spirit of the South, it is often affirmed, was due to the depression that followed the fall of Vicksburg and the defeat at Gettysburg. But it needs little examination to prove that it dates much further back. The Southern people entered into the war in the firm conviction that their antagonists would not fight. The battle of Shiloh rudely dispelled that delusion. Again and again Davis declared that the conflict, in its magnitude, had altogether outrun his expectations. . . .

7. James Ford Rhodes: THE FAILURE TO REALIZE THAT THE NORTH WOULD FIGHT *

The Union of twenty-three States and the Confederacy of eleven were now arrayed against each other. Twenty-two million people confronted nine million, and of the nine million three and a half million were slaves. The proportion was nearly that of five to two. The Union had much greater wealth, was a country of a complex civilization, and boasted of its varied industries; it combined the farm, the shop, and the factory. The Confederacy was but a farm, dependent on Europe and on the North for everything but bread and meat, and before the war for much of those. The North had the money market, and could borrow with greater ease than the South. It was the iron age. The North had done much to develop its wealth of iron, that potent aid of civilization, that necessity of war; the South had scarcely touched its own mineral resources. In nearly every Northern regiment were mechanics of all kinds and men of business training accustomed to system, while the Southern army was made up of gentlemen and poor whites, splendid fighters, of rare courage and striking devotion, but as a whole inferior in education and in a knowledge of the arts and appliances of modern life to the men of the North.

The Union had the advantage of the regular army and navy, of the flag, and of the prestige and machinery of the national government: the ministers from foreign countries were accredited to the United States; the archives of what had been the common government were also in the possession of the Union. The aim of the Confederacy was to gain its independence. Davis, in the message of April 29 to his congress, expressed the sin-

* James Ford Rhodes, *History of the United States,* III (New York: The Macmillan Company, 1895), pp. 284-290.

cere purpose of the Southern people. "We feel that our cause is just and holy," he declared. "We protest solemnly in the face of mankind that we desire peace at any sacrifice save that of honor. In independence we seek no conquest, no aggrandizement, no cession of any kind from the States with which we have lately confederated. All we ask is to be let alone—that those who never held power over us shall not now attempt our subjugation by arms. This we will, we must resist, to the direst extremity." The aim of the North was to save the Union, to maintain the integrity of the nation. The Confederates, the President said in his Fourth-of-July message, "forced upon the country the distinct issue 'immediate dissolution or blood.' . . . It was with the deepest regret, he further declared, "that the executive found the duty of employing the war power in defence of the government forced upon him. He could but perform this duty or surrender the existence of the government." From Davis's message we may clearly see that the doctrine of state-rights would not have been carried in 1861 to the point of secession, had it not been for the purpose of repelling what was considered an aggression on slavery. No one knew this better than Lincoln, but in his message there is not a word concerning the subject, and the reason is apparent. Restricting the object of the war to the restoration of the Union, he had with him Democrats and Bell and Everett men, as well as Republicans; a mention of slavery would at once have aroused the contentions of party.

Many at the South thought that when it came to the supreme test the North would not fight. Assuming even that the Republicans might be ready to take up arms, they believed that the Democrats and conservatives would earnestly oppose an attempt to conquer the seceding States, and so hamper the dominant party that it would be unable to carry out its designs. These became disenchanted as they witnessed the uprising of the North, and bewildered as they saw man after man of distinction on whom they had counted giving in his adherence to the Lincoln government because of the attack on the flag. Had the Confederates foreseen that they would at the very first confront a practically united North, they would have hesitated more than they did to strike the irrevocable blow. Nevertheless, as a large majority be-

lieved in the constitutional right of secession, the war on
the part of the national government seemed to them a
war of subjugation. The North had fastened a stigma on
their property, and when they availed themselves of that
safeguard of the minority which, according to their view,
was intended by the fathers, it tried to compel them by
force to remain in the Union. The Southern literature of
this period is pervaded with two notions which were
fused into the public sentiment: that their fight was for
their property and their liberties, and that it was against
spoliation and conquest. This sentiment, sincerely held
by the statesmen, politicians, and journalists, was trans-
lated into vituperative language to excite the populace.
All held the opinion that the North was unconstitution-
ally and unjustly attempting to make sovereign States do
that which they had deliberately resolved not to do. With
such an idea thoroughly diffused among an Anglo-Saxon
people, one might have known that resistance would be
long and stubborn. The Confederates were by no means
dismayed at the realization of the united North and the
appreciation of the odds of number and wealth against
them. "The numbers opposed to us are immense," wrote
ex-President Tyler; "but twelve thousand Grecians conquered the whole power of Xerxes at Marathon, and our
fathers, a mere handful, overcame the enormous power
of Great Britain." "Has the strongest nation in capital
and population always prevailed in the contest between
nations?" asked the Charleston *Mercury*. "Did Phillip
of Spain or Louis XIV of France subdue Holland? Did
Great Britain subdue our ancestors in 1776?" Nevertheless, in making the effort to gain their independence the
Confederates had undertaken a stupendous task; they
had started out on a road the end of which was at best
doubtful; they had gone to an extreme, before proceeding to which it had been better to endure somewhat of
grievance. Their fight, they averred, was made for liberty,
and yet they were weighted by the denial of liberty to
three and one half million human beings. They had the
distinction of being the only community of the Teutonic
race which did not deem negro slavery wrong; in their
social theory they had parted company with England,
France, Germany, and Italy, and were at one with Spain
and Brazil. . . .

8. Burton J. Hendrick: THE SORRY POLITICAL JUDGMENT OF SOUTHERN LEADERS *

The fact is commonly forgotten that the South possessed civic as well as military figures. It had a government as well as an army. Yet the civilian side has so far attracted little attention from historians. Perhaps the South itself is to blame for this neglect. Significantly its hero of that conflict to-day is Robert E. Lee, not Jefferson Davis. Just as significantly the hero of the North is Abraham Lincoln and not Grant or Sherman. Probably few Americans at the present time could name more than two or three of the seventeen Southerners who served in the Davis Cabinet, while Seward, Stanton, Chase, Welles, and other political captains of the Union are among the most familiar portraits in our national gallery.

Thus does the popular mind, working instinctively, perhaps subconsciously, arrive at a great historic truth. For the fact that the North emphasizes statesmanship in the Civil War and the South military achievement goes far to interpreting the events of 1861-1865. In particular, it may answer a question much debated in that era and since. Why did the South lose the war? Historians on both sides have had a ready explanation for this failure. There is now general agreement that the Southern cause was doomed from the start. The Union's superiority in population and wealth is the commonly accepted reason for its success. In view of the virtual consensus on this point, it is interesting to glance back at opinion contemporary with the Civil War, especially that of Europe. In 1861 and for at least the two succeeding years, European observers also regarded the end as foreordained. Only the judgment of England and the Continent differed from the one almost generally held to-day. In the eyes of Europe in 1861-1863, the North was the side destined inevitably to defeat. Not only military experts, but statesmen, held this conviction. On it the whole diplomatic policy of Europe on "the American question" was constructed. The Federal Union of

* Burton J. Hendrick, *Statesmen of the Lost Cause* (Boston: Little, Brown & Co., 1939), pp. 3-7. Reprinted by permission.

the fathers was at an end. Two republics at least would occupy the area formerly ruled by one; not improbably, four, five, or even more independent nations would rise on the ruins of the Federal Union, thus creating a political system in the northern half of the Western Hemisphere not unlike that which for fifty years had raised havoc in South America.

What was the reason that the statesmen, diplomats, journalists, and historians of England and the Continent took this portentous view of the American Civil War? Why did they regard a Confederate triumph as inherent in the nature of the case? Merely because, as they interpreted history, Uncle Sam had undertaken an impossible military task. Many nations had assumed such problems in the past, and almost all had failed. The circumstance that the North outnumbered the South in population, the fact that its domestic wealth and commerce exceeded those of the Confederacy, did not seem to these experienced observers the ultimate considerations. Indeed, in face of the respective problems confronting the two parties, it was not certain that Northern power so greatly surpassed that of the South. In an absolute sense, of course, the Federal Government unquestionably counted more men, and commanded more resources, than its adversary. But surface ratios like these did not necessarily determine events. The military problems of the two sides were very different, and would have to be weighed in estimating their relative physical might. The fight was an unequal one, if considered merely from the standpoint of men and materials; here the North clearly possessed the advantage. It was similarly unequal, from the standpoint of military strategy, and here the South just as unmistakably wielded the upper hand.

No one knows, and probably never will know, just how many men fought in the Civil War. The Confederacy kept no statistics of any value, and those of the Federal Government, superficially more precise, involve many repetitions. Reliable figures on the population of the two sections exist, and these usually do unwarranted service in attempts to arrive at their respective military strength. In 1860, the states that afterward formed the Confederacy had roughly 9,000,000 souls; those that remained loyal to the Union and contributed to its man power—Maryland, Kentucky, and Missouri, must be eliminated from the calculation—19,000,000. The figures for the South, it is true, comprise 4,000,000 negroes, but these, from the first, increased its military power, for they could provide a service as teamsters, cooks, workers on entrenchments and fortifications—labor that white recruits performed in the Federal army. Negroes also gave the South its supply of laborers and farmers at home, thus freeing the Anglo-Saxon population for military service. Moreover, the blacks comprised a reserve for possible soldiers at the front; the idea of using them for this purpose, naturally revolting to Southern instincts, appealed from the first to many farseeing leaders. In the last two years, General Lee favored the enlistment of colored troops, and in March, 1865, Jefferson Davis himself advocated a bill for such enlistments. The Confederate Congress passed this measure in March, 1865, a few weeks before Lee's surrender.

It is therefore fair to say that the proportion of Northern to Southern men available for war service stood at about two to one. In view of the military problems confronting the two sides, this indicates a proportion rather in favor of the Davis Government. The point is that the North was fighting on the offensive, the South on the defensive. The North was the invader; the South was engaged in repelling its invasion. Abraham Lincoln was waging a war of conquest, and Jefferson Davis was struggling to repel the attack. One side was encroaching on an unfamiliar country, comprising a vast territorial extent and a hostile people, and the other was standing firmly on its own friendly soil, could fight on positions of its own selection, and was engaged in no real effort to subdue the enemy, but merely to beat him off. It is a truism of the military art that success in offensive warfare requires a great superiority in men. The usual estimate places this at three to one. "The numerical preponderance of the North," says a leading English authority, Sir Frederick Maurice, in his book on Robert E. Lee, "was for the purposes of war far less than would appear from an examination of the election returns." The same authority places the proportion of North to South at five to three—somewhat under the two to one estimate above, and considerably inferior to the three to one usually regarded as necessary in offensive warfare.

The performance of the South which the world so greatly admired—that of holding, with half the population, the North at bay for two years—was no new phenomenon. Such exploits are found in all ages. Illustrations in plenty spring at once to mind. One thinks of the Greeks against the Persians; the little island of Queen Elizabeth against the mighty realm of Philip II; the Netherlands against Spain; Frederick the Great in the eighteenth century against the combined powers of Europe; the American colonies in 1776 against Great Britain. A striking case was that of 1792, when the ragamuffin soldiers of the French Revolution defeated and dispersed the finely equipped forces of Prussia and Austria, far outnumbering them. The battle of Valmy bears a certain resemblance to Bull Run, and it was the first step in that conquest of most of Europe ultimately achieved by Napoleon. Perhaps our own time supplies the most astounding instance, that of the two Boer republics of South Africa, with a population of 200,000, resisting the might of Great Britain (45,000,000) and its world empire for four years, from 1898 to 1902. All these powers, like the United States in 1861-1865, were invaders, engaged in conquest, fighting a people numerically weaker, but brave and determined, fiercely employed in the desperate task of defending their own firesides.

The courage and ability of the Southern armies aroused the admiration of their foes; that Southern generalship, at least in the first two years, surpassed that of the North, stands upon the surface; other facts than an inferiority in military strength must therefore hold the secret of Confederate failure. We shall probably find it rather in civil than in military affairs. Had statesmen ruled its domestic and foreign policies with the same skill that Lee and other generals guided its armies, the result might have easily been very different. In one respect this assertion may look like a reversal of history. Statesmanship was a quality on which the South had always prided itself. Its political thinkers had played a leading role in framing the Constitution. For nearly forty years following 1789 it gave the Union its Presidents.

For most of the thirty years preceding the Civil War the South had governed the nation in all three departments. It seems strange, therefore, that at the supreme test of 1861-1865 this region should so disastrously fail in that statesmanship which it had always regarded as almost its exclusive possession. But perhaps there is a solution to the mystery. It may be found in the particular South that organized the Confederacy and plunged the nation into war. The fact to be kept always in mind is that the South which started the Confederacy, and dominated its government for four years, was not the South that wrote the Declaration of Independence, played so important a role in framing the Constitution, and provided so much leadership for the United States in its earliest days.

9. Sir Frederick Maurice: THE FAILINGS OF JEFFERSON DAVIS *

Davis was not a great man, but I believe him to have been above the average of war ministers, and during the first year of the war his experience of affairs in general and of military affairs in particular made him a formidable opponent of Lincoln who had had no such experience. His weaknesses were due to his failure to insist that the interests of the Confederacy as a whole should take precedence of the interests of the individual States, to an excess of caution, and to a tendency to rely too much on his small military experience, which caused him to concern himself with minor details. The first of these weaknesses was inherent in the Southern claim to the precedence of the rights of the States, but Davis appears often to have made little effort to get the States to relinquish their several rights for the common good and even to have gone further sometimes than the States themselves required. One example will suffice. The Confederate law authorised the President to accept contingents from the States but left him free to choose all the

* Sir Frederick Maurice, *Governments and War: A Study of the Conduct of War* (Little, Brown, Boston).

commanders of larger formations than regiments. Esprit de corps would naturally be promoted by keeping troops from the same State together under a commander from that State, but the first essential was that the commander should be efficient. We find Davis writing on October 10th, 1861, to Major-General G. W. Smith:—"Kentucky has a brigadier but not a brigade, she has, however, a regiment, that regiment and brigadier might be associated together. Louisiana had regiments enough to form a brigade, but no brigadier in either corps; all of the regiments were sent to that corps which was commanded by a Louisiana general. Georgia has regiments now organised into two brigades; she has on duty with the army two brigadiers, but one of them serves with other troops. Mississippi troops were scattered as if the State were unknown." [1] There is in this letter and in a number of others of similar tenor no hint that military exigencies should be considered, or that commanders should possess some other qualification than a birthplace in a particular State. Ample evidence exists that Davis was subject to considerable political pressure on these and similar matters, but his position was sufficiently strong, at least in the first years of the war, to have made it possible for him to have explained to his complainants that military requirements must have precedence over sentimental considerations and that such matters must be in the hands of the soldiers. As it was, his time was taken up with these details, which he should have insisted on leaving to his war department, and his generals were worried and sometimes even seriously hampered by untimely requests to change commanders and reorganise troops. Later in the war a number of those generals who had most distinguished themselves proved to be Virginians and in this the influence of Lee, a Virginian, was seen by jealous citizens of other States. There is good reason to believe that the difficulties between Lee and Longstreet, which had very serious consequences for the South, were not remedied by Davis because Longstreet, a gallant man and a good tactician, but a bad subordinate, was a favourite son of Georgia, and the President was fearful of offending that State. This kind of difficulty usually arises when forces have to be raised at the

[1] Davis, "Rise and Fall," Vol. I., p. 445.

outbreak of war. Kitchener has been considerably criticised because he did not use the existing Territorial Force for the expansion of the British army in the great War, but preferred to raise new armies *ab ovo*. The chief factor which influenced him was his memory of the pressure brought by county magnates and persons of influence during the South African War to get units employed at the front which they had raised, or were prepared to raise, according to their fancy, and he feared that similar influences would prevent the development of the systematic organisation which he knew to be necessary.[2] The best way to deal with this matter in a country which has not a system of compulsory service, and in which the general public is therefore usually ignorant of the principles and requirements of military organisation, is to explain it frankly. A public eager to win the war and not lacking in common-sense may be trusted to respond when it knows what is wanted and why it is wanted. If Davis had exercised in this matter the same courage displayed by him in getting adopted the Conscription Act, which might fairly have been considered a violation of State rights, he would have rendered the South a very real service, and incidentally relieved himself of much vexatious labour.

But the Confederate President's desire to foster State sentiment, doubtless for what he believed to be good military reasons, led him to make an even more serious mistake. He organised the Confederacy into military departments, placing a general in command of all troops in each department. Such an arrangement, excellent in time of peace, was fatal in time of war, for the military situation took no account of geographical boundaries, while the departments followed in the main State lines. The Mississippi early in the war was seen by the Federals, with their command of the sea, to be a promising line of attack, but the great river was a dividing line between Confederate military departments, and lack of co-operation between them was one of the reasons why Lincoln was able in July, 1863, to proclaim that "the father of waters goes again unvexed to the sea." Nor was this all, for a great part of the war the only coordinating authority between the several departments was

[2] Arthur, "Life of Lord Kitchener," Vol. III., p. 309.

the President himself, and he had neither the military competence nor the leisure to arrange and direct timely concentration. The consequence of this was that the Confederacy failed to obtain the fullest advantage from its central position, which was the greatest strategical advantage it possessed. When Lee was at Davis' side there was combination, and the first battle of Bull Run was won because of J. E. Johnston's opportune junction with Beauregard. But for a great part of the war Lee was not in Richmond, and combination between departments was then the exception. It is, however, only fair to Davis to say that in 1861 no power in Europe save Prussia had devised an effective system for the provision of military advice to the head of the State in time of war. Davis' military knowledge was sufficient to keep him from interfering save exceptionally with the operations of his generals in the field, his interference being usually confined to matters of organisation and personnel, but that military knowledge was insufficient to enable him to appreciate the difficulties of and the need for unity of direction of forces scattered over a wide area. Failing to understand the difficulties he could produce no solution. Here is one more example of the danger of a little knowledge. Davis' small experience of war had taught him what a name and an association may mean to soldiers. He recalled the pride which his Mississippi Rifles in the Mexican campaign had taken in their name and in their State connexion, and remembered what this had meant in military efficiency. But he did not realise that the command of a battalion in the field might be an inadequate schooling for the direction of a great war. . . .

If it was not possible for the Confederates to advance straight from the field of Bull Run across the Potomac and carry the war into Northern territory, it soon became not only possible but urgently necessary to do this. The North was much depressed by the defeat; the general in command in Washington was expecting and apprehensive of attack.[3] The term of service of the militia, which had been enlisted for three months, and formed a considerable part of the Federal army, had expired and new levies were required to replace it. The North had its difficulties in creating a supply of arms and munitions,

[3] "McClellan's Own Story," p. 87.

and was at this early stage of the war far less well
supplied than was supposed in the South. The loss of a
quantity of war material at Bull Run was therefore a
serious matter. Indeed at no period of the war was the
North so vulnerable, but given time the loss would be
made good, new armies could be created. Clearly then
the policy for the South was to allow the North as little
time as possible for recovery. But it was at this period
of the war that Davis shewed himself to be at his weakest. Lee had been sent off to conduct a difficult campaign
in the mountains of Western Virginia, and the President,
left to himself, was seen to have no policy save to protect as much of Southern territory as might be and hope
for foreign intervention. This was a futile policy; futile
politically, because the border States, Kentucky, Missouri,
Western Virginia, and Maryland, were wavering; they
might be won by enterprise, they would certainly be lost
by inaction; futile militarily, because to give an enemy
with superior resources time to develop those resources
was to make him a present of what he needed most.
The soldiers saw all this. J. E. Johnston, Beauregard,
and Augustus Smith were all agreed that, given reinforce-
ments, which they believed to be available, they could and
should take the offensive. But August slipped by and
September and nothing was done. Then on October 1st
Davis came at Johnston's request to the army for a
conference with his generals. Johnston said he needed
19,000 men to enable him to invade Maryland. Smith
thought 10,000 would suffice. The President answered
that he had not a man to give them. More than the
number Johnston asked for were guarding the coasts
against possible raids by the Federal fleet. That fleet,
weak as it then was, saved the North from a great
danger. In Davis' defence it may be said that there were
risks in weakening the garrisons on the coast. The South
at this time was uncertain and nervous as to the effect
of the war upon the large negro population in its midst.
When the white men went off to the war women and
children were left in the midst of negroes. There were
fears that Federal incursions might be the signal for
servile risings, and the President was inundated with
demands for the protection of exposed points. Davis, who
could never make up his mind to take risks for a great

end, yielded to these demands and adopted a policy of passive defence, which he mitigated with proposals for enterprises of so minor an order that one is amazed to find the head of a State permitting himself to be concerned with such details . . .

There is possibly another reason for Davis' reluctance to give Johnston the troops he needed. He disliked the soldier. That dislike may have originated at Westpoint, where Johnston was a model and Davis but an indifferent cadet. Be that as it may, Johnston, who was Quartermaster-General in the United States army when he resigned from its service, held, not without some reason, that Davis had treated him unfairly in the matter of his seniority in the Confederate army, and expressed his opinion plainly. Davis' answer was brief and discourteous.[4] Lee would never have troubled his head about such a matter, but Johnston was a man of different temper, and Davis, as head of the State, should have been big enough not to have quarrelled with him as long as he wanted to use him. In the event the ill-feeling then begun grew and correspondence between the two shows the existence of friction so constant as to have affected seriously the cause both were serving. Neither of the men were blameless, but of the two Davis is the more blameworthy. He should either not have given Johnston the most important command in the Confederate army, or, having placed him in it, have trusted him. To retain a general in command and bicker with him is not the act of a statesman. Johnston was one of the three ablest soldiers of the South, and Davis' treatment of him is among the less creditable acts of his Presidency.

[4] It ran:—"Sir, I have received and read your letter of the 12th instant. The language is, as you say, unusual, its arguments and statements utterly one-sided and its insinuations as unfounded as they are unbecoming.
I am etc.,
JEFFERSON DAVIS."

10. Bell Irvin Wiley: THE INFLEXIBILTY OF SOUTHERN LEADERSHIP *

An important failure of the Confederacy was the failure of flexibility. Throughout the antebellum period the South had remained predominantly agricultural, rural and provincial, while the North was becoming industrial, urban and national. Millions of foreigners poured into the North in the decades immediately preceding the Civil War, bringing new ideas, new skills and new ways. The flood of immigration, the expansion of industry, the growth of cities and the increase of wealth gave Northern life zestfulness and elasticity, afforded valuable experience in large-scale enterprise and brought to the people an enlarged vision of the nation's greatness and power.

Southern life, on the other hand, relatively uninfluenced by immigration, hemmed in by an intellectual blockade for the protection of slavery and enchained by an agricultural economy, tended to be static, conservative and sectional. To put it another way, Southerners drew back in a shell, assumed a defensive posture, planted cotton, proclaimed the blessings of slavery, denounced Yankees and "furriners" and hoarded the treasures of the past, while the North and other parts of the world, responding to the blandishments of "progress," marched off and left them.

When, in the spring of 1861, the South found itself involved in war, it was a new kind of war: one in which railroads, steamships, massive armies and vast distances played an important role. It was a war which had to be sustained by factories, skilled laborers and trained managers. It called for large-scale activity, close coordination and expert administration. It was modern war. It was big business. Its successful prosecution required varied talents, ready adaptation and the ability to think big thoughts.

Notwithstanding remarkable achievement in many areas of endeavor, the fact remains that the agrarian and provincial South, bound by its old ways and concepts, was not sufficiently flexible to wage a modern war

* Bell Irvin Wiley, *The Road to Appomattox* (Memphis: Memphis State College Press, 1956), pp. 78-84, 85-90, 94-96, 99-102, 113-121. Reprinted by permission.

against the modern nation that its adversary had become.

The South's political leaders did not break away from the localism to which they were tied by custom and preference. State governors in varying degree insisted on organizing troops, appointing officers, hoarding supplies, controlling transportation and influencing military operations within their respective boundaries. Davis was so thoroughly imbued with the doctrine of local rights that he sometimes failed to exercise the central authority conferred upon him by Congress. In April, 1863, the Confederate lawmakers passed an act giving the President virtually supreme control over railroads, but Davis never took anything like full adantage of this important measure. Robert C. Black in his excellent book, *Railroads of the Confederacy*, declares that the President "appeared smitten by a fatal hesitation." "Nearly every carrier represented a state, county or municipal interest," he adds, and "Jefferson Davis found himself enmeshed in the strands of his own (state rights) philosophy."

Provincialism was of course not peculiar to the leaders of the Confederacy. The hold which it had on the people generally is well illustrated by the statement of an upcountry South Carolinian to John W. DeForest after the war: "I'll give you my notion of things," said the Southerner; "I go first for Greenville, then for Greenville District, then for the up-country, then for South Carolina, then for the South, then for the United States; and after that I don't go for anything. I've no use for Englishmen, Turks and Chinese."

In a large measure, owing to widespread addiction to state rights, the Confederacy tried to operate on the basis of eleven separate conflicts instead of merging its resources into one great centrally-directed war.

The setting up of a separate government and the conduct of a great modern war required a proficiency in large-scale administration. The Southern planters, lawyers, bankers and business men who had directed public and private affairs with reasonable success under the old union in times of peace were unable to cope with the new and larger responsibilities thrust upon them by secession and conflict. The capacity for organizing and managing extensive and complex activities was sadly lacking in the Confederacy.

Want of administrative ability was notoriously prevalent among government officials. It was also a salient weakness among generals. The South produced an impressive number of brilliant combat commanders but it had no full general who was outstanding both in battle and in administration. Lee came nearest to achieving distinction in both capacities. But he failed to develop an efficient staff, his orders were sometimes lacking in clarity, and some of his campaigns were poorly coordinated.

The Confederacy's command and staff systems, as Professor T. Harry Williams and others have pointed out, were considerably inferior to those of the North. The South had eight full generals, while the North's top boss consisted of one lieutenant general. But when it came to staff, the group that actually administers an army and coordinates its activities, the Confederacy was shockingly stingy. Lee's staff was headed by a colonel, while that of the Army of the Potomac had several brigadiers and the chief of staff was a major general. The North adopted a unified command in March, 1864, with Lincoln at the top, Grant as general-in-chief and Halleck in between as chief of staff. The Confederacy did not get around to unifying the control of its armies under a general-in-chief until February, 1865, when its cause was doomed.

The direction of Confederate military affairs suffered greatly from looseness and inefficiency throughout the war. In February, 1862, a regimental commander wrote Senator C. C. Clay from Tuscumbia, Alabama: "This valley seems entirely overlooked; (Albert Sidney) Johnston thinks it is in Beauregard's Department; Polk thinks it is in his; but nobody seems alive to its vast importance and few know even where it is." A similar lack of understanding and looseness of management was apparent in the conduct of the Vicksburg campaign. And confusion as to channels of communication and areas of jurisdiction as between Lee, Beauregard, Davis and Bragg greatly impaired operations around Richmond and Petersburg in May and June, 1864. During his incumbency as commander of the Trans-Mississippi Department, Kirby Smith was often troubled by uncertainty as to the extent of his authority.

The inflexibility underlying the looseness and misman-agement that characterized the South's conduct of the war was sharply and vividly expressed by L. M. Keitt, a South Carolina general and ex-Confederate Congress-man, in a series of letters written to his wife early in 1864. On January 22, he wrote: "(I) fear that our people have not risen to the height of this present crisis. . . . They have cherished state pride and exclusiveness for eighty years, and no changes however great, no ruin however appalling, could make them forget it for a moment. Our people will not move out of the old forms and routine."

Two days later he stated: "I wish with us that Genius and the hour were wedded. A planting people are always the victim of routine . . . in war a fatal defect."

On January 31, he observed: "You cannot have liaison, connection, unity among a planting community. . . . We are in mortal peril from our inability to govern ourselves." On February 11, he added: "Countries like ours are not fit for revolution . . . Is it because there is no genius? No, the land is full of it. . . . What is the cause of this? Our political institutions. In peace they make us great through our individuality; in war they make us weak through want of harmony and complete obedience to routine."

If by routine he meant, as he apparently did, slavish devotion to tradition, to an outlook that was limited, to an economy that was agrarian, to ways that were outmoded, he was hitting very close to the truth.

*   *   *

Another failure that helped lead the South down the road to Appomattox was the failure of judgment. This failure can be associated with its isolation and defense complex.

Shut off from the outside world and misled by wish-ful thinking, the South developed exaggerated ideas about its own strength. The thought, as stated in Confederate arithmetics, that one Southerner could whip at least seven Yankees was a silly one, but it did not seem so to the "brave Southrons" who bandied it about one hundred years ago. The people of Dixie in those days had talked so long and so loud of the superiority of themselves and their way of life that they had become victims of their own propaganda.

Southerners erred in their judgment of Europe. Most of them were thoroughly convinced that England, France and other nations were so completely dependent on cotton that they would quickly intervene, if necessary, to maintain the flow of fibre to their mills. They failed to take into account the huge surpluses of cotton and cloth that had accumulated in European warehouses in the period immediately preceding the war. They did not anticipate the resort by the outside world to expedients and substitutes to offset the cotton shortage. They did not foresee the counterbalancing efforts of tremendous profits from the manufacture, shipping and sale to both belligerents of munitions and other commodities essential to war. Finally, they were blinded to the great hostility to slavery among those who would suffer most from the cotton famine, the working classes of the great textile centers. Southerners traveled extensively in Europe in the antebellum period, and they should have sensed that cotton was not king, but they were so habituated to accepting the pleasant and ignoring the unpleasant that they were impervious to the truth.

Southerners also misjudged their foes. They underestimated the North's industrial might and the mood and strength of its teeming population. They thought that Northerners were so cowardly and so deeply concerned with material gain that they would not go to war; and that if they did, a battle or two would convert them to peace. Unaware of the tremendous influence of the rail and water lines that reached out from the East, they firmly believed that the West would not join in the conflict except as an ally of the South. They knew that antislavery sentiment was strong in the North, but they thought it was limited largely to the abolitionist wing of the Republican party. They were grossly ignorant of the enormous hold that this sentiment had on some of the immigrant groups and the strength that it had attained among Democrats.

The most serious error of Southerners in judging their foes was their failure to appreciate the depth of the North's devotion to the Union. In the period from 1820 to 1860 the North's political philosophy had undergone a transformation. The local and sectional outlook that lay back of the Hartford Convention had gradually given way to a strong national consciousness. Many influences had contributed to this evolution among which were the strong nationalistic concepts of some of the immigrant groups and especially the Germans; an increasing realization of the benefits of a strong central government to industry and business; and the growing conviction that America, committed to the principle of freedom and democracy, was destined to be an example and a refuge for liberty-loving people everywhere. Southerners not sharing the experiences which led to the North's conversion to the ideal of Union had little awareness of the revolution that was taking place beyond the Mason and Dixon line. Because of ignorance the Southerner made the mistake first of thinking that the North would not risk a war to prevent the disruption of the Union and second, that it would not make a sustained and costly effort to restore it. Hence, Southern leaders with few exceptions proclaimed independence with light-heartedness and confidence, and after the first great victories looked hopefully to the North for signs of acceptance of separation. Had they realized that thousands upon thousands of young men from Wisconsin, Minnesota, Pennsylvania and Massachusetts and other Northern states were willing to lay down their lives on the altar of Union, and that the folk at home would support them, these leaders probably would not have urged the people to secession, and if they had, they would have been constrained after the South's initial victories to gird them for a long and hard struggle.

But the Southern leaders and their people failed to comprehend the temper of the North and of Europe just as they failed to realize their own weaknesses. And these failures along with those of flexibility, public information, harmony, morale and leadership, were salient influences leading the South down the long and torturing way to Appomattox.

Study of these influences and their bearing on the course of the conflict indicates that the turning point in the struggle came in the spring of 1862 rather than in July, 1863, the usually accepted time. When the combined effects of Fort Henry, Fort Donelson and other military reverses are considered, along with the loss of confidence in leadership, the tremendous decline of public morale, the break between Davis and Congress, the enactment of laws deeply obnoxious to the people such as those providing for conscription and the suspension of habeas corpus—all of which date back to the early months of 1862—it becomes apparent that the South's ability to wage war effectively was severely and permanently curtailed. Its only hope of triumph after the spring of 1862, lay in the collapse of the North's determination to persevere in the struggle. When cognizance is taken of the strength among Northerners of the ideal of Union, the likelihood of such a collapse appears remote indeed. Even if Lee had won at Gettysburg and captured Washington, New York and Philadelphia, it seems extremely doubtful, in view of the North's devotion to the Union, that the outcome of the war would have been other than what it was.

Part V

THE FAILURE TO HOLD
THE BORDER STATES

11. Albert Bushnell Hart: SIGNIFICANCE
OF THE BORDER STATES *

The Southern Confederacy, at the very beginning, encountered a fatal disappointment; it failed to carry with
it four of the slave-holding States, Missouri, Maryland,
Delaware, Kentucky, and a part of a fifth, West Virginia.
These five States, having a combined population of
3,600,000 people, never seceded and never furnished
money by loan or taxation for the Confederate cause;
and the men who entered the Confederate army from
those States were nearly offset by the mountaineers from
Tennessee and North Carolina who entered the Union
Army. The action of a few patriotic men like Holt of
Kentucky, Fletcher of Missouri, and Brown of Maryland,
and the prompt action of Butler and Frémont and Buell
and Grant, in securing a military occupation of those
States, prevented them from throwing in their lot with
the Confederacy. The population of the eleven seceding
States was 8,700,000; the population of the twenty-one
non-seceding States, from Kansas to Maine, was 21,950,-
000. Instead of the odds of population being three to two
in favor of the North, they were thus made five to two.
With proper military management, aided by a spirited
support from the Northern people, the defeat of the
South was therefore physically possible; indeed, defeat
was likely. Nor was this the only advantage gained by
the North through its relations with the border States
in 1861. The theatre of war was thrust further south.
The possession of Kentucky and Missouri enabled the

* Albert Bushnell Hart, "Why the South Was Defeated in
  the Civil War," *Practical Essays on American Government* (New York, 1893), pp. 270-271.

northern troops to block the entrance to the Tennessee and to the Missouri Rivers; and the military occupation of the border States, which were justly assumed to be lukewarm in their support of the Union, made it possible to return from those States members of Congress who did not represent their people; thus was insured that compact majority in Congress which supported the President, pressed forward the war, urged through the constitutional amendments, and completed the process of reconstruction. When Virginia, in April, 1861, responded with a defiance to the President's call for troops, she did it because she understood, as Von Holst has well said, that she belonged either to hammer or anvil, and she preferred to strike rather than to receive a blow. Though the secession of Maryland, Kentucky, and Missouri was prevented, those States could not remove the war from their borders; but their strength was lost to the weaker party, if not wholly transferred to the stronger. . . .

12. Edward Conrad Smith: THE FATAL LOSS OF THE BORDER STATES *

The response of Kentucky to the events beginning the war, in complete contrast to the state of public opinion in western Virginia and Missouri, showed that the cause of the Union was in a precarious situation. It was not so because public opinion held the North responsible for the outbreak of hostilities, for President Lincoln's carefully formulated policy in regard to Fort Sumter effectually disarmed his opponents in the State, and the sturdy defense of Major Anderson, a native of Kentucky, aroused the admiration of all classes. The correct explanation seems to lie in the fact that sentimentally the people had always considered themselves as Southerners. Upon the outbreak of the war they therefore, without much consideration of questions of right or wrong, or of national or state politics, felt impelled to join in

* Edward Conrad Smith, *The Borderland in the Civil War* (New York: The Macmillan Company, 1927), pp. 263-265, 273-279, 282, 284-285, 293, 294, 297-299, 311-312, 388-391, 394-395. Reprinted by permission.

the defense of their section. Probably only the sentiment of devotion to the Union, which moved them in the opposite direction, prevented them from beginning a course of action that, upon sober second thought, they must have regretted. In the first few months following the outbreak of the war, Kentucky was unsteadily balanced between the Union and the Confederacy.

The unconditional Union party in the State was much weaker than in Missouri, and the active secessionists were much stronger. They were, in fact, so strong and so actively engaged in manufacturing sentiment favorable to their cause that it might have appeared to an outsider that the whole State had turned secessionist. On the day of the surrender of Fort Sumter Blanton Duncan mobilized a regiment which he had enrolled for the Confederate army. When he later paraded it through the streets of Louisville, thousands of citizens lined the sidewalk, waving goodbys and cheering for the soldiers and the cause in which they were engaged. On April 15th Governor Magoffin telegraphed in response to the President's call for troops: "I say emphatically Kentucky will furnish no troops for the wicked purpose of subduing her sister Southern States." The action of the governor was outwardly approved by everyone, though some of the unionists ventured to criticize the wording of the refusal. In Louisville, on April 18th, a mass meeting attended by three thousand persons not only approved the reply, but declared that Kentucky should not allow Federal troops to be marched across her territory for the purpose of attacking the Confederate States. If war should come, it was resolved that Kentucky ought to share the destiny of the South. At Paris, a meeting condemned the conduct of the national government and approved Magoffin's course. From Lexington, John H. Morgan wrote to the Confederate government, tendering twenty thousand men to "defend Southern liberty against Northern conquest." A few days later John C. Breckinridge lent his powerful influence to the secessionists, declaring publicly at Louisville that the President's course was illegal, and recommending that the people of Kentucky make one more effort at mediation in the halls of Congress. If they should fail in this, he thought it their duty to unite with the South. In only two sections of the State—in the counties opposite Cincinnati and in the sparsely settled mountainous region—was there an immediate rallying of the people to support the Union. It is probable that if a convention had been in session when the news from Fort Sumter was received, it, like the convention in Virginia, would have passed an ordinance of secession. . . .

Naturally the people throughout the State were tremendously interested in the session. Many of them sought in various ways to bring pressure to bear upon their representatives. The Union leaders were more active and more clever in organizing this sort of activity than their opponents. From nearly every county in the State petitions, signed by thousands of women, were presented praying for the preservation of peace through neutrality. It is said that these petitions were circulated by unconditional Union men. Many citizens, of course, thronged to Frankfort to watch the proceedings. No sooner would an influential secessionist group appear than the telegraph would summon equally influential Union leaders from Louisville, Covington and other centers to reinforce the unionist lobby already at the capital. By such means as these the supporters of the national government succeeded, by the narrowest of margins, in dominating the proceedings.

The critical point came near the middle of the session, after a desultory series of divisions in which the Union party had had a majority of one. Someone proposed to lay on the table a substitute for a secessionist resolution. It was a matter of little or no practical consequence, but of the highest parliamentary importance. When the vote was taken, the question was declared rejected by a majority of one. A Union member had gone over to the opposition. The secessionists exulted over their victory, for their success at last seemed assured; but on the very next vote the member returned to his party allegiance. The occurrence seemed to take the spirit out of the secessionists, who shortly afterward abandoned their hope of being able to accomplish their purpose at that session. They accepted instead the principle of neutrality by legislative act.

There still remained a question as to the form of neutrality which Kentucky should adopt. Should she merely request the belligerents to respect her territory, and depend upon their good faith to do so, or should she arm herself to prevent violations? The legislature decided in favor of armed neutrality, against the opposition of some Union members who were unwilling that the State Guard should be further strengthened. Since the session of the legislature in the winter its enlisted personnel had grown to fifteen thousand men. From the beginning of its organization, complaints had been frequently heard that the state authorities were discriminating against the enlistment of Union men. They were accused of having accepted many secessionist companies which had not complied with the terms of the law, while preventing the enrollment of unionist companies which had done so. It was generally known that nearly all the officers and men were of secessionist leanings. The organization was therefore regarded as a menace to the cause of the Union.

In order to counterbalance its power and secure an armed force that would protect the interests of the Union and of Union men against it, many companies of home guards were organized throughout northern and central Kentucky. Near the beginning of the legislative session, Lieutenant William Nelson had surreptitiously brought into the State five thousand muskets which he had obtained from the War Department at Washington. These so-called "Lincoln rifles" were distributed among the home guards by night. By the middle of the session there were two distinct military organizations in the State, of not unequal strength. Both were prepared to defend Kentucky against external aggression, though they watched for enemies in different directions.

When the Union leaders found it impossible to prevent the granting of appropriations for the military, they determined to safeguard the funds from being used wholly for the benefit of the secessionists. General Buckner's estimates for the State Guard were greatly pared down. Instead of the $3,000,000 which he asked for, the legislature appropriated $750,000 for equipment and training, half to be spent for the State Guard, and half for the Union home guards. The disbursement of the funds was taken out of the hands of the governor and vested in a commission of five members, a majority of whom were Union men, named by the legislature. Furthermore, it was provided that the home guards should not be called into the service of the State;—in other words, that the governor, who was the commander-in-chief of the militia, should be debarred from exercising control over half the military establishment supported by the State. Finally, a provision was inserted that none of the arms and equipment supplied by the State should be used against either the United States or the Confederate States except to repel invasion.

After the Union leaders had thus succeeded in tying the hands of the secessionists and in getting so great a degree of control for themselves, they seemed somehow to lose interest in the question of neutrality. The secessionists, on the other hand, now insisted upon it. They succeeded in having each house pass a resolution of strict neutrality; but owing to the opposition of the Union members, they were unable to secure the concurrence of both houses on any single measure. The result was that the only official pronouncement of the position of Kentucky was an executive proclamation by Governor Magoffin.

There can be no doubt that the neutrality of Kentucky was advantageous to the Southern Confederacy from both a political and a military standpoint. As Lincoln said in a later message to Congress, its consequences would be "disunion completed." For if one State could repudiate its obligations to the national government while remaining in the union, it was difficult to show why other States might not secede. It was a most far-reaching application of the doctrine of state sovereignty, since it crippled the national government in its efforts to enforce the laws in the regions where resistance occurred. "At a stroke," said Lincoln, "it would take all the trouble off the hands of secession, except only what proceeds from the external blockade. It would do for the disunionists that which, of all things, they most desire—feed them well, and give them disunion without a struggle of their own." Still, he did not think it wise to interfere in the affairs of the State, contenting himself with measures to encourage the Union party which had a tendency toward only peaceful penetration.

On May 7th Colonel Robert Anderson, Kentucky's and the nation's hero of Fort Sumter, was assigned to the duty of raising volunteers for the Union army from western Virginia and Kentucky. He thoroughly understood the sentiments of the people and was in full sympathy with the plans of Garrett Davis and the other Union leaders. From his headquarters in Cincinnati he exercised a great deal of influence over the course of public opinion in the State. Another native of Kentucky who rendered a great service for the Union was Lieutenant Nelson of the Navy. At the beginning of the war he had expressed a preference for returning to his State and trying to save it from secession, rather than for treading a quarter-deck. His plan was approved by President Lincoln, who gave him a leave of absence and allowed him to go to Kentucky without instructions. One of his first acts was to obtain arms from the War Department and distribute them among the home guards. During the next two months he traveled throughout the State, holding conferences with unionist leaders and making preparations for more aggressive . . . action when the proper time came.

All along the northern bank of the Ohio River, Governors Dennison, Morton and Yates had established posts to prevent the shipment of arms and military supplies to States that were not completely supporting the Federal government. Camp Defiance, at Cairo, was particularly effective in enforcing the embargo, cutting off nearly all the trade of western Kentucky and Tennessee. As a result, serious complaint arose among the people of Kentucky, which threatened to develop into rebellion. Notwithstanding the evident danger of losing the State, the restrictions were kept in effect until President Lincoln took control of the regulation of trade and relaxed the embargo. An immense trade with the South at once grew up on all the routes through Kentucky. The southward-borne shipments of foodstuffs and materials of war taxed the capacity of the Louisville and Nashville Railroad. . . .

On the day of the interview between Buckner and McClellan, the Border States Conference met at Frankfort, with delegates present from the western slave States that had not seceded. The proceedings failed to attract a great deal of attention outside of Kentucky, and the conference has been all but forgotten. But the results were extremely important in their influence on public opinion within the State. The resolutions declared that there was no warrant for secession in the Constitution and no justification for it in the facts existing when the Southern States seceded; that the obligations of the people to the Constitution and the national government remained unimpaired; and that no changes in the fundamental law should be made except only the addition of a constitutional amendment guaranteeing the protection of slave property in the four slave States which still remained in the Union. The delegates from Kentucky issued a separate address to the people, recommending that their State should again appear in the Congress of the United States and "insist upon her Constitutional rights in the Union, not out of it."

The purpose of the address was to influence public opinion in the campaign for members of Congress, who were to be chosen at a special election on June 20th. After the adjournment of the legislature this was the next most important trial of strength between the secessionist and unionist parties. . . .

The results of the election must have been a surprise even to the most sanguine Union men. Their candidates were successful everywhere except in the first congressional district, which included the western counties of the State along the Mississippi and in the lower valleys of the Cumberland and Tennessee rivers. Even there the Union candidate received forty-one per cent of the total vote. In the Blue Grass region, where slaves were most numerous, the people gave the majority of their votes to the Union ticket. In the eighth congressional district, embracing the towns of Paris, Lexington and Frankfort, the Union candidate received only fifty-nine per cent of the total; but the party ticket was successful in all the other districts by overwhelming majorities. Only five counties in the eastern part of the State—Owen, Harrison, Scott, Anderson and Morgan—gave majorities for the States' Rights candidates. Daviess and Logan were the only other counties outside the first congressional district in which they had a majority. . . .

An interesting feature of the result is the relation which it discloses between Union sentiment and slave-holding. Woodford County, where the slaves outnumbered the white population, gave a majority to the Union candidate. In every one of the seven other counties in which the slave population was more than forty per cent of the total the candidates of the party were successful, their votes being in some cases two or three to one. The counties in which the secessionists were strongest were not important slaveholding counties at all. Of the four which gave the States' Rights candidates more than three-fourths of their total vote, only one had a slave population of more than twenty per cent. Generally speaking, it is safe to state that the presence of slaves had little influence on the course of public opinion. What influence it had seems to have been exerted on the side of the Union. . . .

Just at this particularly favorable moment in the affairs of Kentucky, the cause of the Union was placed in serious jeopardy by the stupid and high-handed act of a Federal general in a neighboring State. Fremont, possibly trying to build up his political strength among the extreme anti-slavery group at the North, issued an order, on August 30th, providing that the slaves of citizens of Missouri who had taken up arms against the United States should be liberated upon their application to the military authorities. The report of the action created consternation among the Union men of Kentucky, who had built up their following by stressing the fact that the war was being fought only to reunite a divided country. . . .

President Lincoln thoroughly appreciated the dangers of the situation and the importance of holding Kentucky in the Union. "I think to lose Kentucky," he wrote a little later, "is nearly the same as to lose the whole game. Kentucky gone we cannot hold Missouri, nor, as I think, Maryland. These all against us, and the job on our hands is too large for us. We would as well consent to separation at once, including the surrender of the capital." On September 2nd, he wrote to Fremont requesting him to modify his proclamation so as to render it less offensive to the loyal people of the border slave States. Upon Fremont's refusal to do so, Lincoln himself ordered the necessary changes. The incident was soon forgotten among the events that followed. It is nevertheless important in showing the temper of public opinion in Kentucky and the dangers to be anticipated from a single misstep on the part of even a subordinate. . . .

[*On the Confederate side*] the delicate question of dealing with Kentucky was left wholly to Polk, who, although a soldier and a churchman of distinction, was no politician. Six days after [*Polk's occupation of Columbus, Kentucky,*] he wrote to Magoffin, almost casually informing him of his recent movement, which he justified by quoting Davis's opinion as to military necessity. He declared his willingness to withdraw his forces, providing, first, that the Federal troops be withdrawn simultaneously, and secondly, "that the Federal troops shall not be allowed to enter or occupy any part of Kentucky in the future." Coming from the commander whose movements were chiefly responsible for the presence of Grant's forces in the State, these were arrogant demands. In dealing with a legislative committee which was later appointed to confer with him, his attitude was even more unfortunate. He committed the unpardonable political sin of attempting to justify his acts before the people of Kentucky by pointing out their own violations of neutrality. Among other things, he charged that the State had allowed the national government to seize at Paducah property belonging to citizens of the Confederacy, and to cut timber from her forests for the building of gunboats. Though both these allegations were true, they were hardly sufficient to justify an invasion before the bar of public opinion in Kentucky. A third charge that the establishment of Camp Dick Robinson constituted a violation of neutrality was easily answered, since it was only necessary to point out the fact that Confederate sympathizers had also established recruiting camps in the State. When Polk further called attention to the fact that representatives of Kentucky in the Congress of the United States had voted supplies of men and money to carry on the war, he exposed, better than had yet been done, the fallacy of the doctrine of neutrality. A State could not be neutral and remain in the Union. In presenting the issue thus clearly, he played directly into the hands of the Union party.

The attitude of the Confederate authorities toward Kentucky brought to completion a realignment of political groupings within the State. After the August election the more advanced Union men looked forward to having Kentucky definitely support the national government. The conservative members of the party and the secessionists were content to continue the policy of neutrality. But after the Confederates entered Kentucky, the pro-Southern minority were left alone, struggling to achieve some arrangement whereby the former policy of the Union men could be continued. Like the Confederate authorities, however, they failed utterly to sense the revolution in public opinion until it was too late to warn their friends in the South. A States' Rights convention at Frankfort on September 10th contented itself with resolutions deploring the unnatural war, advocating neutrality and the dispersal of the Federal camps in the State, and offering to help drive out the Confederates as soon as the Union troops had left. . . .

It is hardly too much to say that the decision of Kentucky was the determining factor in the war. It lent aid and encouragement to the Union men of Tennessee and Missouri. It consolidated the cause of the United States in the southern part of what is now West Virginia, making it possible to extend the boundaries of the new State southward with the consent of most of the people. It opened the way into the heart of the Confederacy, making possible the later Union campaigns in Tennessee. South of the Ohio River there was no good line of defense for the Southern armies. From the time that Kentucky finally made her decision for the Union, they fought a losing battle. If the Confederate government in September, 1861, had realized the importance of the neutrality of Kentucky, and had treated the State with the respect to which it was entitled, it is possible that the Union armies would not have been able to use her soil as a base against them. If, on the other hand, the national government had committed one-fifth of the blunders it had in Missouri, Kentucky would almost certainly have sided with the South. A President of the United States who was unfamiliar with conditions in the State would probably have made mistakes. Abraham Lincoln understood the temper of the people better than any other statesman of his time. He realized that he could not force the issue, but must give the people time to make up their minds and fix their own course.

There are few better instances of his statesmanship than the manner in which he dealt with the situation in Kentucky and, indeed, in the whole of the Ohio Valley in the critical year of 1861. Jefferson Davis, in contrast, though a native of Kentucky like Lincoln, threw away the chances of his government to survive through his inability to understand the temper of the people and to deal with them diplomatically. . . .

The problem of both the Union and the Confederate governments in dealing with the Borderland was diplomatic, rather than purely political, in character. The solidarity of sentiment made advisable the adoption of a program which would appeal to the whole section; and the considerable acceptance of the doctrine of States' rights made necessary carefully conducted negotiations with the authorities of the States. The prize was well forth striving for. If the North were to conquer the seceded States, it must secure the active cooperation of the Borderland. If the South were to succeed in its movement for independence, it must secure its support, or at least its continued neutrality. Each section had good reason to be hopeful of the result. The people of the Borderland were Southern in origin, and therefore could be expected to maintain a sympathetic attitude toward the South. Their trade, throughout most of their existence, had been with the port of New Orleans, and the force of commercial habit was still influential. Their disapproval of the purposes and methods of the extreme abolitionists was well known. On the other hand, the economic and social organization of the Borderland was nearly similar to that of the North. The old barrier to free intercourse had been broken down by the construction of the railroads, with the result that a community of commercial interests between the two sections had quickly developed. And the popular disapproval of the militant pro-slavery movement in the South had just been expressed in the election of 1860. To all appearances the forces were nearly equally balanced. The issue depended upon the future measures taken by the government concerning the matters in which the Borderland was peculiarly interested.

In dealing with the situation, Lincoln showed far more acumen than Davis and other Southern leaders, first, in

estimating correctly the position of the people of the
Borderland, and secondly, in seizing upon the issue to
which, in the greatest degree, they were susceptible. If
he had based his policy upon the rights of a downtrodden
race, as another Republican President might have done,
he would have had the North with him, but he would
have lost the Borderland and with it, all hope of re-
establishing the Union. He was extremely careful not to
make this the issue. Instead, he risked having only the
lukewarm support of the North by appealing, from the
beginning of his administration, almost solely to the nationalist sentiments of all the people. In relieving Fort
Sumter, he took the greatest possible precaution to show
that he did not intend to attack any State, but only to
keep possession of a fort which belonged to the national
government. He made it plain that if war occurred it
would have to be inaugurated by the South in firing upon
the flag of the United States. The outcome won for the
national government the support of all the States of the
Borderland except Missouri and Kentucky; and even in
Missouri, only a small faction actively aided the state
authorities in their resistance. In his relations with Kentucky, he conceded points, he tacitly recognized an assumed neutrality, and he delayed important military operations, all out of deference to the feeling of States' rights
which existed there. He showed such a disinclination to
favor emancipation as to provoke an abolitionist gibe
that "Mr. Lincoln would like to have God on his side,
but he must have Kentucky." The Southern leaders, on
the other hand, utterly failed to grasp the essential nature
of the situation. They adopted an intractable and dictatorial policy, finally ending in a foolish invasion of the
State which turned it toward the active and powerful
support of the Federal government.

After the people of the Borderland had made their
decisions and, on an impulse of glowing patriotism, had
pledged men and money to defend the Union, the problem was by no means solved. There still remained the
danger of reaction, of a sudden cooling of ardor, which
would have been as calamitous as the assumption of a
neutral position from the beginning. As Lincoln said,
the people must have their pride enlisted, must want to
beat the rebels. It was therefore necessary that the na-

tional government continue to conduct the war solely on
the issue of union against disunion, and that it give the
responsible leaders in each State the greatest possible
latitude in the determination of purely local questions,
interfering only when they went too far. . . . In pur-
suance of this policy the Restored Government of Virginia was recognized, and West Virginia was later admitted as a State. Through the wise advice of the leaders
in Kentucky, the State was allowed to occupy a completely neutral position over a period of several months,
during which secret propagandist activities gradually
turned the people toward the Union. Only in Missouri
was the confidence in the judgment of the leaders mis-
placed. Their over-aggressive policy would have been
disastrous if the mass of the people had not been so
strongly imbued with nationalist sentiments that they
were able to overlook flagrant attacks upon the dignity
of their State.

It may be well to point out again that the course taken
by the people of the Borderland exercised a decisive influence over the history of the country during the period
of the Civil War. In the beginning, when many people in
the North showed a disinclination to do anything toward
preserving the Union, they threw their whole strength
into an effort to secure a peaceful settlement of the
difficulties. Though they failed, they were yet successful;
for they effectually halted the secessionist movement, and
they gained time for the development of nationalist sentiment everywhere except in the South. When the war was
begun by the Confederate States, they devoted themselves with rare zeal to the single purpose of restoring
the authority of the national government. Their voluntary enlistments were greater in proportion to population
than those of other sections, and the draft was necessary
among them at a later date. Even when the issue of the
war was apparently changed by the proclamation of
emancipation, they were wise enough not to be turned
away from the main object they had in view. They continued to support the armed forces of the Union until
the military strength of the Confederacy was destroyed,
and the authority of the United States was again extended
over all parts of the country.

Part VI

THE FAILURE OF DIPLOMACY

13. James H. Hammond and Alexander H. Stephens: COTTON IS KING

Senator James H. Hammond of South Carolina, speech in the Senate, March 4, 1858:

If there were no other reason why we should never have war, would any sane nation make war on cotton? Without firing a gun, without drawing a sword, should they [*the North*] make war on us we could bring the whole world to our feet. . . . What would happen if no cotton was furnished for three years? I will not stop to depict what everyone can imagine, but this is certain: England would topple headlong and carry the whole civilized world with her, save the South. No, you dare not make war on cotton. No power on earth dares to make war upon it.

Alexander H. Stephens, Vice President of the Confederate States, speech on November 1, 1862:

I was in favor of the Government's taking all the cotton that would be subscribed for eight-per-cent, bonds at ten cents a pound. Two million bales of last-year's crop might have been counted on. This would have cost the Government a hundred million bonds. With this cotton in hand and pledged, any number short of fifty of the best iron-clad steamers could have been contracted for and built in Europe—steamers at two millions each could have been procured. Thirty millions would have got fifteen. Five might have been ready by the 1st of January last to open one of our blockaded ports. Three could have been left to keep the port open, while two could have conveyed the cotton across, if necessary. Thus, the debt could have been paid with cotton at a much higher price than it cost, and a channel of trade kept open until others could have been built and paid for in the same way. At less than one month's present expenditure on our army, our coast might have been cleared. Besides this, at least two million more bales of the old crop might have been counted on; this, with the other, making a debt in round numbers to the planters of two hundred million dollars. But this cotton, held in Europe until the price shall be fifty cents a pound [*it went much higher*], would constitute a fund of at least one billion dollars, which not only would have kept our finances in sound condition, but the clear profit of eight hundred million dollars would have met the entire expenses of the war for years to come.

14. Charles H. Wesley: THE FAILURE OF COTTON DIPLOMACY *

The belief was general among Southerners in 1860 that cotton would be the controlling factor with European nations during its struggle with the North. It was asserted that about one-fifth of the British people depended upon the manufacture of cotton for a livelihood, and the opinion that the economic life of England would be paralyzed by a sectional struggle, which would involve cotton was generally accepted by the Southern leadership. This opinion had been growing for a number of years. It was frequently expressed during the fifties that cotton was a real monarch, a king.

The English people found themselves by 1840 unable to secure an adequate supply of raw cotton from either Egypt, India, Brazil, or the West Indies. From this time to the Civil War, four-fifths of British imported cotton came from the Southern states. The cotton fiber of the South was finer, and at the same time cheaper for the British manufacturers. The costs of transportation from sources other than the South were higher and the dangers of damage and loss were also greater. A writer to the

* Charles H. Wesley, *The Collapse of the Confederacy* (Washington, D. C.: The Associated Publishers, Inc., 1937), pp. 106-110, 116-117, 118-120. Reprinted by permission.

London Economist acknowledged that cotton from the Southern states was preferred to cotton from India. He stated (1) that Indian cotton yielded more waste, that is, it lost more in the process of spinning and that it was unusually full of dust and dirt; (2) Indian cotton was shorter in staple and the same machinery would yield from ten to twenty per cent more yarn from American cotton; (3) the spinners could turn out more of American cotton because it was less subject to breaking; and (4) although Indian cotton was of excellent color, it would not take a finish as well and was likely to have a thin appearance after washing. As a whole, it was thought Indian cotton was an inferior article as compared with American cotton. The same paper stated also, "The lives of nearly two million of our countrymen are dependent upon the cotton crops of America; their destiny may be said, without any kind of hyperbole, to hang upon a thread. Should any dire calamity befall the land of cotton, a thousand of our merchant ships would rot idle in docks, two thousand mills must stop their busy looms; two thousand mouths would starve for lack of food." The *London Times* regarded the effects of the war situation directly when it asserted that "so nearly are our interests intertwined with America that civil war in the States means destitution in Lancashire."

Since Great Britain had twice as many spindles in its cotton factories as the rest of Europe, it was estimated that the disasters there would be greater. In France there were similar indications of dependency on the South; but the cotton industry in France was not as extensive in proportions as it was in England, although there were 700,000 workers in France who were said to be dependent upon cotton. It seemed by 1850 that the economic life of these industrial countries would be seriously crippled if their cotton supplies were cut off. The prevalence of this opinion induced the South to conclude that with the opening of the war, England, France or some other European country would either recognize the government of the South or interfere in its behalf. Paul du Bellet, a Louisianian who lived in Paris during the war, characterized the official position of the Confederate government when he wrote that "the President and his advisers entertained the opinion that King Cotton would command the guns of European fleets and whip the United States."

These ideas concerning the dominance of cotton were frequently expressed in current articles and addresses. One boldly asserted in 1861 that secession would be peaceful "because England, France and the rest of commercial Europe, and the Western and Northern states of the Union require that it should be. The world must have the South's cotton at any price." Another writer expressed the confident opinion that the blockade would be broken by the English fleet which would protect English commerce and "especially the free flow of cotton to the English and French factories—a stoppage of the raw material from the cotton states of the South either by failure of crops or civil war and its consequences would produce the most disastrous political results, if not a revolution in England." Senator Iverson of Georgia in his farewell speech to the Senate stated in reference to the blockade, "We can live, if need be, without commerce, but when you shut out our cotton from the looms of Europe we shall see whether other nations will not have something to do on that subject. Cotton is king and it will find means to raise your blockade and disperse your ships." The doctrine that "Cotton is King" occupied a major place in the thought and speech of the Southern people by 1861, and Southern statesmen believed beyond all doubt that England or France would be compelled to recognize the South as an independent power or face industrial ruin. . . .

The smallest supply of cotton for this period was transported to Europe in 1862, and it was in this year that it was hoped the cotton famine would be felt. By July, 1862, the stock on hand in England was reduced to 200,000 bales, and in December the climax was reached. Unemployment and hard times had reached their worst stage. In 1863, however, the European cotton supply was increased to 2,325,000 bales, and in the following year there was a further increase to 2,683,000 bales. These increases were due to additional supplies from India, China, Brazil, and Egypt, and from the development of blockade running.

It was not until late in 1862 that Southern statesmen began to realize that the limitation of cotton exports would not bring about recognition by England and France. The limitation of cotton began then to be relaxed. This is shown by the increases of cotton exportation in 1863 and 1864. The need for war supplies was so great that cotton was smuggled through the blockade in order to secure the desired materials. Efforts to restrict exportation were accordingly discontinued. In spite of this fact, the destruction of the crop by burning large and small amounts was continued in order to reduce the supplies which would reach England through the North. Faith in the power of cotton with Europe ceased to be a factor in Southern resistance after 1863. . . .

The cotton famine with which the Confederacy expected to bring Europe to its feet in 1861 or 1862 did not work out according to order. During the years of large cotton crops in 1859 and 1860, there had been heavy exportations to Europe. Nearly two million bales of American cotton were exported annually to Great Britain between 1858 and 1860. It has been estimated that England had manufactured and stored in its warehouses 300,000,000 pounds of cotton above the demands of normal production. France also had an enormous stock of cotton which had been purchased from the crops of 1859 and 1860. The warehouses of India and China were filled. The result was a surplus from the overproduction and overstocking of the markets. On December 31, 1861, there were 702,510 bales of cotton reported in the English warehouses and 143,345 bales in stock in France. It was said that this was more than the normal two years' supply which was usually kept on hand. In fact, it was estimated that there was a three years' supply in the warehouses. Not only was there a plentiful supply of raw cotton but there was an overproduction of fifty per cent of manufactured cotton goods due to the introduction of machinery for spinning and weaving cotton in the decade preceding the war.

On account of this supply on hand in England, the cotton famine did not take place until the winter of 1862-1863, although in 1862, Mason reported to Benjamin that the famine was increasing in the manufacturing districts, and was attracting serious attention. Mason later explained that recognition was delayed because the manufacturers had large stocks of cotton on hand and that it was not until 1863 when their stocks were being reduced that they began to be favorable toward recognition. He wrote in the summer of 1862 that when the question was presented in the form of unemployment "the causes which withhold cotton from America will be pressed in our favor with increased force on the public attention."

The decrease of the cotton supply was not the only factor involved in the situation. Over-production by the mills had led the British owners of the smaller mills to close their plants or to run them on a part time basis, during the autumn of 1861. In 1862, unemployment and distress made their appearances among the operatives in the cotton manufacturing districts. On July 4, 1862, it was said that 80,000 workers were employed and 370,-000 were only half employed. The total loss in wages was 139,000 pounds. The decline of the English cotton industry continued until the close of 1862. In the spring of 1863, there were improvements, as American cotton began to be brought through the blockade and other supplies arrived from abroad. The shipping of cotton to the northern states and the exhaustion of the manufactured cotton goods influenced prices and led to the normal operation of the mills. The French experienced a similar reduction and cessation of their mills, but after 1862 their situation began to improve. Southern statesmen had expected that the famine would have its climax sooner in the war.

Several new factors introduced themselves in 1863 and changed the consequences of this situation. One was the revival of the linen and woolen industries, which began to bring in larger profits as the war progressed. The rise in these industries served to take up some of the slack in the cotton industry. It was stated that from 1862 to 1864 the linen industry gave employment to over 100,000 new operatives, many of whom had been formerly employed in the cotton mills. Yet as late as 1864, Emperor Napoleon III is reported as saying that "his people were suffering through the scarcity of cotton and were likely to suffer still more." Napoleon delayed, however, in proceeding to recognition or intervention because of the attitude of England and his desire not to provoke a war either with Europe or the United States.

On September 22, when President Lincoln had announced that he would issue an Emancipation Proclamation on January 1, 1863, a new factor was injected into the international situation. . . .

15. Frank Lawrence Owsley: WHY ENGLAND DID NOT INTERVENE *

Looking back over the unfolding of events, it will be seen that the chief diplomatic efforts of the commissioners were directed toward intervention in some form. At times the intervention which they sought was to take the form of repudiation of the Federal blockade, which unquestionably was a violation of the Declaration of Paris and to which the Confederacy had partially subscribed; at other times it was mediation on the principle that the combatants had reached a stalemate; then at other times when the South seemed to have won crushing military victories it was the recognition of independence; and at moments when the interests of Europe were badly injured by the continuance of the war it was to be armed intervention. Underlying the diplomacy of the Confederate States in behalf of intervention was the King Cotton doctrine that Europe must have southern cotton or perish. This King Cotton philosophy, we have seen, was a fairly reasonable one, for about a fourth or fifth of England's population gained its bread from the cotton industry (based principally on the southern supply), and one-tenth of England's wealth was invested in this industry and nearly half of her export trade was made up of manufactured cotton goods. France was not as involved as England, yet the cotton industry, based largely on American cotton, was her largest and most profitable industry, and there were about a million restless operatives including their families engaged in this industry.

The surplus stocks on hand in England and France in 1861 staved off the cotton famine until 1862. This was

* Reprinted from *King Cotton Diplomacy* by Frank Lawrence Owsley, 1931, pp. 562-578, by permission of The University of Chicago Press.

a disappointment to the South, for such a contingency had not been anticipated. But by the combination of the Confederate embargo and a Federal blockade a cotton famine was finally produced in England and France in 1862 which threw over half the operatives out of employment and forced them and their families, amounting to two millions in England and one million in France, upon charity. The Confederacy was very confident of securing intervention as a result of this famine; and the question was seriously canvassed in both the French and the English cabinets in the fall of 1862, but nothing came of it. Then there was in 1863 another serious effort of the Confederate commissioners and their friends to induce England and France to intervene, which ended in the absurd Roebuck-Lindsay episode. During this interval the Confederacy had continued to rely upon the need of Europe for southern cotton to move England and France into intervention. However, the faith in cotton was rapidly weakened after the fall of 1862 when intervention did not come and the cotton famine began to grow less acute. But two other probable forces which might operate in favor of English and French intervention revealed themselves to the Confederate commissioners in the meantime, and they began to stake success heavily upon these two motives after the approaching failure of King Cotton. These were the extreme hatred and jealousy shown in England against the United States as a powerful rival, and the desire of Napoleon to establish a vassal empire in Mexico. These had operated more than all else to throw the sympathies of Napoleon and of the majority of the English upon the side of the South. The appeals of the commissioners for European aid, whether in the building of a navy or in recognition of armed intervention, took cognizance more and more of the desire of England and Napoleon to divide and weaken the United States.

But, as we have seen, neither England nor Napoleon ever raised a hand in aid of the Confederacy, to get cotton or to divide the country. What are the explanations? Why did King Cotton fail to move these powers as had been anticipated? Why did not the desire for weakening a powerful and hated rival bestir England and Napoleon? The answer as far as Napoleon is concerned is simple and may be disposed of briefly. This despot, we will recall, was always eager from the beginning until the end of the American war to join England in intervention. On the other hand, he was under no circumstances willing to intervene alone or in company with weaker powers. He had been perfectly frank with Slidell and Rost in admitting that he refrained from repudiating the blockade or from recognizing the independence of the Confederacy because of his apprehension that the United States would declare war on him should he do so. While he had a powerful navy of ironclads, he was fearful of the results of a war with America. The reasons for his fear were many: It was not just America alone which he feared in case of war, but most of Europe, he thought, would be on his back. There were Prussia, Russia, Austria, Sardinia, and even England who would welcome such a war to close in upon him from the rear, and he knew it and constantly adverted to the subject in his conversations with Slidell and others on the question of intervention. However, there was another force which he feared equally as much—the disapproval of the French people of a war with America. We have observed that the French people were in sympathy with the North because of the fact that the South was slaveholding and because of the traditional friendship of the French for the United States, and especially because of the universal desire to see the United States grow strong as a counterpoise to England. Napoleon's American policy was diametrically opposed to traditional French policy and sympathies, and he himself was as unpopular with the French as was his policy. Should he bring on a war with America, even with his foreign enemies quiescent, he might lose his throne. He could not hazard a war with America, or if he did it must be in company with England, his chief ally and deadliest enemy. He always stood ready to join England in intervention. Barkis was willin'.

Let us, then, see why England did not bow to the command of King Cotton and break the blockade, or recognize the Confederacy, or meddle in some way with the struggle so as to assure herself of a supply of cotton and the permanent division of a too-powerful rival. First, let us examine the King Cotton question, and explain the spectacle of twenty six members of Parliament from

Lancashire and eight or ten from Lanarkshire, Derbyshire, and Leicestershire—the cotton districts—and especially from Liverpool, sitting silently, apparently bored with all questions of intervention, only one, in fact, Hopwood, ever showing any real interest in the question; and of hundreds of thousands of operatives with their families upon charity, losing $200,000,000 in wages without revolting.

How England and especially the industrial population resisted the power of King Cotton has two usual explanations—though other factors are conceded as playing minor parts. The older school has placed England's non-intervention upon a high and idealistic basis: the sympathy of the Lancashire population—and of the common people generally—with the Union as a great experiment in democracy, as a great model which was held up to the English; and their antipathy to slavery. The newer school of economic historians has not been satisfied with such high motives for mere cotton-mill workers; they have insisted that the antidote for one economic impulse is to be found in another and greater economic impulse. This antidote for the King Cotton virus has been found in a simple name which bears no royal trappings like King Cotton. It, in fact, had until 1861 been the scullion in King's Cotton's kitchen or at most a buck private in the rear ranks of this sovereign—the name referred to is "wheat." England must have American wheat or perish.

These two motives together or separately are inadequate explanations of why England did not intervene to obtain cotton. The idealistic theory of the sympathy of the Lancashire population with the North as a sole explanation is too good to be true. The agitations and mass meetings held in England by William Forster and John Bright and by other less radical northern propagandists, and the vast multitudes who voted petitions to Parliament and cabinet against intervention, have been taken too much at their face value, while similar agitations and mass meetings and giant petitions got up by James Spence, William Lindsay, Roebuck, Beresford-Hope, and other southern propagandists have been too much ignored. The fact of the whole business is, as we have seen, that these meetings, whether pro-northern or pro-southern, were not spontaneous, but were drummed up by well-subsidized leaders and were frequently packed by the liberal use of small coin. The population of Lancashire and of all industrial England was politically apathetic, sodden, ignorant, and docile, with the exception of a few intelligent and earnest leaders. They wanted bread, they wanted clothes, they needed medicines to give their sick children and aged parents, they wanted pretty clothing for their daughters and sisters who were being forced into prostitution. One is not surprised, therefore, to learn from the correspondence of Mason, Spence, Henry Hotze, and others that the purchasability of these people was a coldly recognized fact which the pro-northern and pro-southern agitators made use of. Under these circumstances the public meetings and agitations of the Federal and Confederate sympathizers would be largely determined by the use made of slush funds. This gave the edge to the northern agitation, perhaps. Another factor already noted which would still further give the appearance of greater sympathy for the North than for the South was the fact that Bright and Forster could always with perfect timeliness raise a town meeting, a petition, or a resolution against intervention, while James Spence and his cohorts could hold a mass meeting or pass a resolution favoring intervention only when the military situation was overwhelmingly in favor of the South.

John Watts, connected with the committee for the relief of the Lancashire population and a native of that section, expressed the opinion in his *Facts of the Cotton Famine* that the population of Lancashire was pretty evenly divided in their attitude toward the Civil War. But be that as it may, whether the population was evenly divided or all on the northern side, it is doubtful whether they exercised much influence upon the non-intervention policy of the British government. Few of these people wielded the vote, so the government had little to fear from them in a political way; and there is no evidence to show that the government feared that they would refuse to support a possible war with the United States should England decide to intervene. The fear lay in the opposite direction. The government, in fact, was convinced that the only danger lay in this population's forcing England into war with the United States to obtain cotton. This fear was not great, however, as Palmerston knew his docile and submissive British workmen. They required only enough to keep body and soul together, and the wealth of England saw that they had just this much and no more. As John Bright remarked, it would be cheaper to feed these workers on champagne and venison than to have them force England into intervention, but it was found necessary to feed them only with bread and water. These people then, did not count in a political way, and, as long as they could be kept from insurrection, they would not count in any other respect as far as the government of Palmerston and Russell was concerned.

What about the more recent economic interpretation, the influence of wheat in keeping John Bull on his good behavior with the United States? In this interpretation it is pointed out that England suffered from a very short grain crop in 1860-61-62, and that the great deficiency was supplied by the wheat and grain of the United States, just at the time when Parliament and the cabinet were considering the question of intervention to get cotton; and that the probability or certainty of a wheat famine in case England should become involved in a war by intervention prevented the British government from taking action. It is true that William E. Forster, John Bright, and a few others conducted a considerable agitation in and out of Parliament against intervention, partly on the supposed dependence of England upon American wheat and grain. But outside of the industrial districts this doctrine made no impression. Parliament and the House of Lords did not think enough of it to discuss it, and complete silence on the subject reigned in the cabinet circles. No mention has been found in official or private correspondence of these men which would indicate that a wheat famine would accompany a war with the United States.

This silence would not be conclusive were there not other evidence of a more positive character which corroborates this negative evidence. In the first place, the wheat-famine idea can be identified as Federal propaganda emanating from William H. Seward and Abraham Lincoln. As we have seen, in the fall and winter of 1861-62 Seward wrote several dispatches to Adams and Dayton, at the time when rumors of intervention were causing the American people great alarm, warning England and France that while they might have a cotton famine now they would suffer both a wheat and a cotton famine if they interfered with the struggle in America. Charles Francis Adams was on intimate terms with William Forster, and there is definite evidence to show that he read or paraphrased some of these dispatches to that gentleman who in turn passed the good word on to Bright. In the meantime, Seward indoctrinated Charles Sumner and the latter was soon writing about it to Bright and his other British friends.

The British press, however, with few exceptions, sneered at the idea. Both the *London Economist* and the *London Times* touched upon the fatal point, namely, that the assumption was made without foundation that Great Britain could not get wheat elsewhere than the United States, when as a matter of fact Great Britain's deficiencies could be easily supplied in many other places, including Poland, Russia, and Prussia. The large purchases from the United States during the years 1860, 1861, and 1862, amounting in 1862 to almost half the total importation, were, according to the *Times,* matters of mere convenience of transportation and a slightly cheaper purchase price, not of necessity. Most important of all, it was pointed out that England took this wheat in payment for the countless millions of dollars' worth of rifles, cannon, powder, and other munitions of war which she was selling the United States. In fact, the North, now that cotton could no longer be shipped to England, had no other means by which it could purchase its munitions abroad. No other medium of international exchange existed, and it was pointed out with much truth that the United States would be bankrupt if its wheat were cut off by war, and its munitions of war would be so curtailed that it would have been defeated by the South alone.

This contention of the *Times* and other papers seems convincing, especially in view of the fact that in 1864 and 1865, after the United States became practically self-sufficient in the production of war supplies and no longer made large purchases from England, the latter country turned abruptly away from America to Russia and East Europe for her wheat supply. Recent researches in the

British archives disclosed no concern with a wheat famine; the explanation that American wheat was cheaper and served as the chief medium of international exchange for British munitions of war, and the proof of this in the abrupt cessation of purchases of wheat when the munition trade ceased, all tend to demonstrate that wheat had little if anything to do with preventing English intervention in the American Civil War.

What, then, is the answer to the question as to why England did not intervene to obtain cotton? One must admit the correctness of the principle laid down by the economic interpretation group of historians, namely, that in order to counteract one economic impulse another stronger economic motive is necessary. But it is difficult to see that wheat was a strong element in the economic impulse which counteracted the King Cotton impulse. It is proposed to substitute a much more sinister term for wheat—*"war profits."* Those who are at all familiar with the war profits in the last war ought not to have any great difficulty in grasping the role England played of war profiteer, and the powerful influence upon government of her war profiteers, especially when all, even the small fish, were prosperous as a result of the war.

Perhaps the most surprising of the war profits was in the cotton industry itself. The warehouses of India, China, and of England, as has been observed, had a surplus that it would take two years to consume were no other good manufactured, and England had on hand in her warehouses 700,000 bales more than the normal surplus of raw cotton. The raw cotton had cost around fourteen cents a pound, and the manufactured goods stored in warehouses could not be sold at the cost of the raw material: The British industry was faced with bankruptcy. The mills were already beginning to slow down before the war, and British financial and economic writers were predicting a long period of unemployment and suffering for the operatives. Then the Civil War came as if in answer to prayer and cut off the supply of cheap cotton. The price of raw cotton rose from fourteen cents to sixty, and as time passed the surplus manufactured goods followed suit until at length everything was sold at a net profit of not less than $200,000,-000. In the meanwhile, the larger and well-financed mills continued to manufacture goods and hold against the rising markets: These larger mills, which Arnold estimates as composing two-thirds of the industry, not merely made a profit out of this vast surplus of cheap pre-war goods, but averaged a neat profit on their output over the four years of war. The only people who went down were the small mill-owners and the cotton operatives. They lost all they had. But the industry was saved from one of the worst panics in history, and impending ruin turned into undreamed-of profits. No wonder the members of Parliament from Lancashire sat silently during the debates on intervention. Instead of desiring intervention these members of Parliament and the industrialists they represented must have been praying that the Lord would see fit to let the Civil War continue forever. This attitude is well illustrated by one of the small cotton-buyers who had bought a few-score bales and was holding them against a rising market when the news reached England that Sherman had captured Savannah with perhaps 30,000 bales of cotton. This Englishman, with all his small fortune tied up in these few bales of cotton, on hearing of this news exclaimed: "If that news should come true, some one would ha' to stick to him" lest he commit suicide! Every peace rumor or rumor of captured cotton, says Watts, brought a panic and "good and honorable men spoke of the probable cessation of the most terrible war of modern times as a thing to be dreaded." As paradoxical as it may seem, even the operatives who were working, when at all, on short time, with a total loss of wages almost equal to the war profits of their employers, shared in the apprehension of peace. Each peace rumor, each rumor that the government was discussing intervention sent the price of cotton down and caused the shutdown of small mills whose owners had been caught on narrow margins or who were unable to manufacture in the hopes of future profits. The operatives were caught in a vicious circle. They could not hope for full-time work during the war, but they were afraid that when the war ended they would lose their jobs entirely. Not only were the mill-owners and cotton-buyers involved in this speculation, but the banking interests of England were directly and indirectly concerned. To these men who had made big profits and had refinanced the cotton industry upon the basis of high-priced raw cotton the end of the war meant a flood of cheap cotton, and that meant Judgment Day. James Spence wrote that to these men, though they were in entire sympathy with the South, "the idea of recognition was that of heavy instant loss,—a very formidable obstacle in the way" of recognition.

There is another phase of the cotton profits which must not be overlooked, namely, the development of India as a rival source for raw cotton. England, as we have seen, had tried for twenty or more years before 1860 to rehabilitate the Indian cotton industry in the face of American rivalry with little success, but the elimination of the American crop was India's opportunity. The *London Times* rejoiced that "American cotton is actually out of the running—and there is no saying how long it may continue so," "and when America appears in the market again India ought to be her match. If this can be accomplished, England will be relieved from any risk of another cotton drought." "It would have been difficult," commented the *Times* some time later, "to beat America out of the market, but America is out of the market by her own act. Before she comes in again, there will be time, in all probability, to organize a new trade, and though we must be sorely straitened in the interval, it may be hoped that the result will finally emancipate us from difficulties which had been foreseen and dreaded." Great hopes were expressed that the American monopoly might be overthrown. Some were optimistic enough to believe that the American staple might be permanently eclipsed; others were of the opinion that as soon as the war ended the cheap American supply would drive all other cotton out; while perhaps the majority thought that if the war lasted long enough India would at least share equally in the world-market with American cotton. Certainly the Indian supply made great strides during the war. We will recall that before the Civil War from 80 to 85 per cent of the British and European supply of cotton came from America. But the war cut off the bulk of the American supply, and England turned at once to India. In 1862 Great Britain imported 3,505,844 hundredweight of cotton from India out of a total importation of 4,676,333 hundredweight; in 1863 she imported 3,878,758 hundredweight from India out of a total importation of 5,978,422 hundredweight; in 1864 she imported from India 4,522,560 hundredweight out of a total of 7,975,935 hundredweight. And when the war ended England was getting 85 per cent from India. Nor did the end of the war bring an immediate end to the increase, for in 1866 England imported 2,000,000 bales, or 6,000,000 hundredweight (the Indian bale weighed 300 pounds) from India, and it was still believed that the American market could never again reduce the Indian supply to less than 2,000,000 bales, or about 50 per cent of the British supply. The failure of this prophecy has no part in Civil War diplomacy.

The next great sources of profits are closely related to the cotton industry—the profits which were reaped from the linen and woolen industries, the old rivals of cotton. These two textile industries, which had languished since the Industrial Revolution, waked to life again and recaptured much of their lost ground and reaped a golden harvest. The linen industry responded instantly to the rise in the price of cotton. In 1858 there were only 91,648 acres in flax in Ireland—the chief source of supply—whereas in 1864 there were 301,942 acres under this crop, or an increase of 229 per cent. The production increased from less than 20,000 tons to above 80,000 tons during this time, or 300 per cent. The importation of flax was increased about 20,000 tons. The importation of yarn increased from 58,866 pounds in 1861 to 3,997,106 pounds in 1863. The output of the mills was increased almost as much as were the exports of certain products. The export of yarns increased from 27,981,042 pounds in 1861 to 40,510,967 pounds in 1864 —44 per cent; the export of thread increased from 2,390,461 pounds in 1861 to 4,030,365 pounds in 1864, or about 68 per cent; the export of plain cloth increased from 116,322,469 yards in 1861 to 209,859,714 yards in 1864, or about 80 per cent. The domestic sale of linen was also greatly increased.

It is estimated by John Watts in his *Facts of the Cotton Famine* that during the three years 1862, 1863, and 1864 the linen industry realized 14,500,000 pounds above the normal profits covering an equal period before the Civil War. For 1865 the excess profit continued and carried the figures up above 20,000,000 pounds, or nearly $100,000,000. Watts also estimates that 100,000 extra operatives and laborers were employed as a result of this expansion of the industry, thus taking up much of the slack caused by the slump in employment in the cotton industry.

The woolen industry netted a larger profit than did linen, distributed from farmer to manufacturer. In 1861 the export of the chief woolen products was about 160,-000,000 yards while in 1864 it had increased to 240,000,-000 yards, or 50 per cent increase. A similar increase in domestic sales took place. Watts estimates the excess profits to the manufacturers in the three years 1862, 1863, and 1864 at 17,000,000 pounds, and the profits for 1865 may be put at 5,000,000 pounds. The same writer estimated the excess profits the farmers received from raw wool at 8,932,286 pounds—carrying the excess profits in the woolen industry above 30,000,000 pounds, or $150,-000,000. As in the linen industry there was great increase in the number of operatives, estimated at between 50,000 and 100,000.

Another business which waxed fat and greasy upon war conditions was the munitions industry. The United States for two years and the Confederacy for the entire war bought most of their small arms, cannon, powder, lead, steel plate, rails, knives, sabers, and bayonets from Europe and especially from England. From 1861 to 1864, $7,027,730 worth of alkali-saltpeter, kanit, etc.; about 3,000,000 small arms, or $25,000,000 worth; 30,000,000 pounds of powder, or $10,000,000 worth; $3,000,000 worth of lead; $10,000,000 worth of unwrought steel; $3,000,000 worth of boiler plate, $5,000,000 worth of artillery, to mention only the most important war supplies, were recorded as exported to the United States and the Confederacy. It is certainly a conservative estimate based upon the Board of Trade reports to say that the North and the South bought together no less than $100,000,000 worth of war supplies from Great Britain. This is exclusive of clothing, tents, shoes, and leather goods.

Nor does it include the sale of ships and steamers to the Confederacy or the building of steamers for English blockade-runners. This last item is of great importance, for it stimulated very greatly the shipbuilding industry. Altogether about four hundred steamers, many of them iron, and eight hundred sail vessels were sold as blockade-runners. Great numbers of these vessels were constructed during the war. In addition to this, six ironclads and two wooden cruisers were constructed by the shipbuilders of Liverpool and Glasgow for the Confederate government.

Attention is called to the enormous profits which the blockade-running houses made in that business. Between a million and a million and a half bales of cotton were run through the blockade at a net profit of seldom less than 300 per cent. Goods shipped into the Confederacy, exclusive of munitions which formed only a small portion of this trade, netted a profit frequently amounting to 500 per cent. One round trip through the blockade frequently paid for a vessel and its cargo and left a profit. Many of these vessels, it will be recalled, ran scores of times, the "Little Hattie" making about sixty trips.

But the greatest profit of all, one which was so enormous it cannot be measured in dollars and cents, was made possible in the complete destruction of the American merchant marine directly or indirectly by the Confederate privateers and cruisers. This destruction was done without England's lifting her hand, except in a benediction upon the Confederacy for doing her work so thoroughly. In 1860 the United States was and had been for many years England's only serious rival in the world-carrying trade. So successful, in fact, had been the United States that she had largely driven England out of the direct trade between America and Great Britain—the most sensitive point of all. The United States had in this trade in 1860 2,245,000 tons and Great Britain had only 946,000, while the total ocean-going tonnage of the American merchant marine was between 5,500,000 and 6,000,000 tons, practically as large as that of Great Britain and doubling every ten years. Its ships were magnificent. They could outsail anything afloat. The "Yankee Clipper" had been the despair and envy of the world. In 1861 England saw this magnificent fleet of seabirds begin to scatter and then disappear, until when the war ended only a little over a million tons of culls, mostly coasting vessels which could not be sold, were left, and, as Admiral Porter remarked sadly, the American merchant marine was virtually extinct. The cruisers and privateers had sunk or captured above two hundred ships, destroying around thirty million dollars' worth of property. But their greatest havoc was wrought by indirection. The hazard was so great that marine insurance rose higher than it was in the war with England in 1812 when that power had our coast blockaded, and shippers and merchants, American as well as European, were so fearful of the work of the "Alabama" and her sisters that they could not be induced to ship their merchandise on American ships.

So the magnificent ships lay in dock swinging idly at their cables, their crews scattered, and their sails and hulls rotting while less worthy craft plied the seas. Nothing was finally left except to sell them to neutrals whose flag would make them safe. England got the best and the greatest number. By the first of July, 1864, all had been sold of this great fleet except 1,674,516 tons, mostly obsolete and coasting vessels; and England had already bought over $42,000,000 worth out of a total sale of $64,799,750. This sale continued, as we have said, until little more than 1,000,000 tons of scraps were left. England's only rival had been destroyed for an indefinite span of years. England has fought wars for less than the destruction of a rival's merchant marine. Surely England could keep the peace for such a magnificent reward—especially since war would mean the destruction of her own merchant marine, in a similar fashion.

We see, therefore, that England far from being hagridden by poverty during the American Civil War made enormous material profits. Her surplus stock of cotton was sold at a fabulous profit, her linen and woolen industries reaped unexpected harvests of gold, her munitions and steel industries enriched themselves, her shipbuilding was enormously stimulated by the demands of the Confederate government and the blockade business, merchant houses made millions out of blockade-running, and finally the American merchant marine was driven from the seas and largely transferred to England. An examination of the volume of British imports and exports and the pauper list during the Civil War is rather eloquent of this profit, despite the fact that much of the imports were the invisible earnings of the greatly enhanced merchant marine which do not appear on the books. The total imports were:

1860	210,500,000 pounds
1861	217,500,000 pounds
1862	226,000,000 pounds
1863	249,000,000 pounds
1864	269,000,000 pounds

The total exports including re-exportation were:

1860	164,500,000 pounds
1861	159,600,000 pounds
1862	166,200,000 pounds
1863	196,000,000 pounds
1864	240,000,000 pounds
	(estimated)

That is, the volume of foreign trade in 1864 was 509,-000,000 pounds as against 374,500,000 pounds in 1860, or 34 per cent greater than before the war. There had been a temporary shock in 1861 with the upset of the American markets, but this was largely gained back after that and markets elsewhere especially in France greatly expanded.

An examination of the Poor Law Board reports shows that despite the fact that at one time over a half million people were on the dole in Lancashire the average of those dependent upon charity for all England and Wales was little if any higher during the four years of the American war than during a like period before 1860. For the ten years before 1860 there was an average of about 925,000 people on charity in England and Wales. During the Civil War, despite the increase of the population for these ten years previous, the average number receiving charity was about 975,000, which was little if any larger percentage of the population than before the war in America. This corroborates the statement that the slack caused by cotton operatives being out of work was taken up by the greater productivity of the linen, woolen, munition industries and the expanding merchant marine and the shipbuilding. Even with Lancashire unemployed the labor situation was normal—which meant that outside the cotton districts it was far above normal.

The *London Times* in summing up the situation remarked that "outside of Lancashire it would not be known that anything had occurred to injure the national trade. That is the most extraordinary and surprising incident of the story. An industry which we conceived to be essential to our commercial greatness has been utterly prostrated, without affecting the greatness in any perceptible degree. We are as busy, as rich, and as fortunate in our trade as if the American war had never broken out, and our trade with the states had never been disturbed. Cotton was no king, notwithstanding the prerogatives which had been loudly claimed for him." England could dispense with the cotton industry, so it seemed. John Watts, writing at the same time, remarked that not only could England do without the cotton industry, but "that so far as the people who pay income tax are concerned Lancashire itself seems as if it could almost do without its staple industry," since those incomes seemed unimpaired by the war. *So we may conclude, with regard to the economic motive for intervention: it did not exist.* With the exception of the Lancashire operatives all was well and God was in his heaven!

If the King Cotton basis of diplomacy proved unsound, what about the political motive that England had in desiring a division of the Union? Why did not she intervene to accomplish that greatly desired end? The answer to this is that in the first place England never doubted until it was too late that the South would win its independence and the roast pigeon would thus fly into the open mouth of the British lion without any other effort than the opening of his jaws. This confidence in the southern success has been frequently alluded to in this volume and it has been well presented in E. D. Adams' *Great Britain and the American Civil War*, so it is only necessary to call attention to it here. It was almost a universal belief. In the second place, had this belief not existed the British government could not have been induced to interfere with the American struggle because of a conviction that it would involve the two countries in a war in which, as Bright said, England would be the most vulnerable nation in the world. This is a fear which was constantly expressed by cabinet, Parliament, and press. It was feared that England would lose Canada, and it was absolutely a certainty that she would lose her entire merchant marine, just as the United States was losing its. Certainly she would lose all the great war profits of which we have just spoken. In fact, we might venture to suggest that the economic motive not to intervene outweighed what we might call the political motive of weakening a military and national rival. Finally, there were certain considerations of international laws which would have very strong bearing in preventing England from meddling with the struggle. Had England harbored no fear of war nor loss of her profits she might have refrained from taking any part. She did not wish to help establish a precedent of interfering in a domestic struggle—while war was still flagrant—especially of a first-class power. That privilege was reserved to backward third-rate powers. Again, as we have seen, the Palmerston government hoped to disarm American protests at a later date by allowing that country to establish a paper blockade, and thus vitiate the Declaration of Paris with regard to blockades. Those who recall the British practices of the World War will realize how valuable the precedent was.

Part VII

THE BLOCKADE AND UNION NAVAL POWER

16. James R. Soley: THE ROLE OF THE BLOCKADE *

The success of this undertaking, so unprecedented both in its magnitude and difficulty, can best be judged by the results. The number of prizes brought in during the war was 1,149, of which 210 were steamers. There were also 355 vessels burned, sunk, driven on shore, or otherwise destroyed, of which 85 were steamers; making a total of 1,504 vessels of all classes. The value of these vessels and their cargoes, according to a low estimate, was thirty-one millions of dollars. In the War of 1812, which has always, and justly, been regarded as a successful naval war, the number of captures was 1,719. But the War of 1812 was waged against a commercial nation, and the number of vessels open to capture was therefore far greater. Of the property afloat, destroyed or captured during the Civil War, the larger part suffered in consequence of the blockade. Moreover, in the earlier war, out of the whole number of captures, 1,428 were made by privateers, which were fitted out chiefly as a commercial adventure. In the Civil War the work was done wholly by the navy; and it was done in the face of obstacles of which naval warfare before that time had presented no example or conception.

As a military measure, the blockade was of vital importance in the operations of the war; and it has been commonly said that without it hostilities would have been protracted much longer, and would have been far more bitter and bloody than they were. Its peculiar importance

---

* James R. Soley, "The Blockade and the Cruisers," *The Navy in the Civil War,* Vol. I (New York, 1883), pp. 44-45.

lay in the isolation of the Southern States and in their dependence upon the outside world for the necessaries of life. The only neutral frontier was along the Rio Grande; and the country, for many miles on both sides of the boundary, offered few facilities for trade or transportation. All supplies must come from the seaboard; and the purely agricultural character of Southern industry made supplies from abroad a necessity. Had the position of the two opponents been reversed, and an efficient blockade maintained against the Northern ports, it would have told with far less severity than at the South.

Besides the exclusion of manufactured goods, and especially of munitions of war, which was one of the prime objects of the blockade, its second and equally important object was to prevent the exportation of cotton, with which at this time the Southern States supplied the world. The amount of floating capital at the South was never large; land and slaves were the favorite forms of investment; and the sale of cotton was therefore the main source of income. When exportation was cut off, the Government was deprived of its revenues for the war, and the people of the very means of existence. . . .

17. Admiral French E. Chadwick: THE BLOCKADE *

It has been as a rule, taken for granted that the South was worsted in a fair fight in the field. This is so in a moderate degree only; for the fight was not wholly a fair one. Difference of forces in the field may be set aside, as the fight being on the ground of the weaker, any disproportion in numbers was largely annulled. But the army of the North was lavishly equipped; there was no want of arms, food, raiment, ammunition, or medical care. Everything an army could have the Federal forces had to overflowing. On the other hand the Southern army was starved of all necessaries, not to speak of the luxuries which the abounding North poured forth for

* French E. Chadwick, "The Federal Navy and the South," *Photographic History of the Civil War,* Vol. I (1911), pp. 90-98.

its men in the field. The South was in want of many of these necessaries even in the beginning of the war; toward the end it was in want of all. It was because of this want that it had to yield. General Joseph E. Johnston, writing General Beauregard in 1868, said truly: "We, without the means of purchasing supplies of any kind, or procuring or repairing arms, could continue this war only as robbers or guerillas." The Southern army finally melted away and gave up the fight because it had arrived at the limit of human endurance through the suffering which came of the absolute want brought by the blockade.

Some few historians have recognized and made clear this fact, notably General Charles Francis Adams, himself a valiant soldier of the war. Another is Mr. John Christopher Schwab, professor of political economy in Yale University. The former, analyzing six reasons for the South's failure, given by a British sympathizer in Blackwood's Magazine for July, 1866, says: "We are . . . through elimination brought down to one factor, the blockade, as the controlling condition of Union success. In other words that success was made possible by the undisputed naval and maritime superiority of the North. Cut off from the outer world and all exterior sources of supply, reduced to a state of inanition by the blockade, the Confederacy was pounded to death." The "pounding" was mainly done by the army; the conditions which permitted it to be effectively done were mainly established by the navy.

"The blockade," says Mr. Schwab in his "Financial and Industrial History of the South during the Civil War," "constituted the most powerful tool at the command of the Federal Government in its efforts to subdue the South. The relentless and almost uniformly successful operations of the navy have been minimized in importance by the at times more brilliant achievements of the army; but we lean to ascribing to the navy the larger share in undermining the power of resistance on the part of the South. It was the blockade rather than the ravages of the army that sapped the industrial strength of the Confederacy."

The South was thus beaten by want; and not merely by force of arms. A nation of well on to 6,000,000 could never have been conquered on its own ground by even the great forces the North brought against it but for this failure of resources which made it impossible to bring its full fighting strength into the field. . . .

What has been said shows how clear was the rôle of the navy. The strategic situation was of the simplest; to deprive the South of its intercourse with Europe and in addition to cut the Confederacy in twain through the control of the Mississippi. The latter, gained largely by the battles of Farragut, Porter, Foote, and Davis, was but a part of the great scheme of blockade, as it cut off the supply of food from Texas and the shipments of material which entered that State by way of Matamoras. The question of the military control of Texas could be left aside so long as its communications were cut, for in any case the State would finally have to yield with the rest of the Confederacy. The many thousand troops which would have been an invaluable reenforcement to the Southern armies in the East were to remain west of the Mississippi and were to have no influence in the future events. . . .

Four Unionist objectives were clear. The greatly disaffected border states which had not joined the Confederacy must be secured and the loyal parts of Virginia and Tennessee defended; the southern ports blockaded; the great river which divided the Confederacy into an east and west brought under Federal control; and the army which defended Richmond overcome. At the end of two years all but the last of these objectives had been secured, but it was nearly two years more before the gallant Army of Northern Virginia succumbed through the general misery wrought in the Confederacy by the sealing of its ports and the consequent inability of the Southerners to hold their own against the ever increasing, well-fed and well-supplied forces of the North. To quote again the able Englishman just mentioned, "Judicious indeed was the policy which, at the very outset of the war, brought the tremendous pressure of the sea power to bear against the South, and had her statesmen possessed the knowledge of what that pressure meant, they must have realized that Abraham Lincoln was no ordinary foe. In forcing the Confederates to become the aggressors, and to fire on the national ensign, he had created a united North; in establishing a blockade of their coasts he brought into play a force which, like the mills of God, 'grinds slowly, but grinds exceedingly small.'" It was the command of the sea which finally told and made certain the success of the army and the reuniting of the States. . . .

18. Charles Francis Adams: THE BLOCKADE CUT OFF MATERIEL OF WAR *

When, in April, 1865, Jefferson Davis, after his flight from Richmond, met, at Greensboro', North Carolina, Joseph E. Johnston, then in command of the army confronting Sherman, a species of council was held at which the course to be pursued, in the then obviously desperate condition of affairs, was discussed. Johnston, knowing well the condition of things, and the consequent feeling among his men, when appealed to for his opinion bluntly said that the South felt it was whipped, and was tired of the war. Davis, on the other hand, was eager to continue the struggle. He insisted that in spite of the "terrible" disasters recently sustained, he would in three or four weeks have a large army in the field; and, further, expressed his confident belief that the Confederates could still win, and achieve their independence, if, as he expressed it, "our people will turn out."

That Davis even then honestly so thought is very probable; and, looking only to the number of fighting men on each side available for service under proper conditions, he was right. And yet under existing conditions he was altogether wrong. As respects mere numbers, it is capable of demonstration that, at the close of the struggle, the preponderance was on the side of the Confederacy, and distinctly so. The Union at that time had, it is said, a million men on its muster rolls. Possibly that number were consuming rations and drawing pay. If such was the case, acting on the offensive and deep in

* Charles Francis Adams, "Mr. Rhodes's Fifth Volume," *Proceedings, Massachusetts Historical Society,* 2nd series, Vol. XIX (1905), pp. 320-323.

a vast hostile country, the Union might possibly have
been able to put 500,000 men in the fighting line. On
the other side, notwithstanding the heavy drain of four
years of war, the fighting strength of the Confederacy at
the close cannot have been less than two-thirds of its
normal strength. The South should have been able to
muster, on paper, 900,000 men. Such a force, or even
the half of it, acting on the defensive in a region inadequately supplied with railroad facilities,—and these, such
as they were, very open to attack,—should have been
ample for every purpose. Texas alone had in 1860 a
white population larger by nearly 100,000 than the white
population of the Transvaal and Orange Free State combined in 1899. Texas covered an area of 265,780 square
miles, as against the 161,296 of the combined African
republics; and this vast region was rendered accessible
in 1861 by some 300 miles of railroad, or about one
mile of railroad of most inferior construction to each
900 square miles of territory. The character of the soil
made heavy movement, slow and difficult always, at times
impossible. In such a region and under such conditions,
how could an invading force have been fed or transported, or kept open its lines of communication? Thus,
on the face of the facts, Davis was right, and the South,
if it chose to defend itself, was invincible.

And here we find ourselves face to face with one of
the greatest of the many delusions in the popular conception of practical warfare. In his remark at the Greensboro' conference about the South "turning out," Jefferson Davis seems to have fallen into it. The South, at
that stage of the conflict, simply could not "turn out."
So doing was a physical impossibility. It was Napoleon
who said that an army was like a serpent, it moves on its
belly. In dealing with practical conditions in warfare,
it has always to be borne in mind that an army is a most
complex organization; and its strength is measured and
limited not by the census number of men available, but
the means at hand of arming, equipping, clothing, feed-
ing and transporting those men. Mere numbers in excess
of those means constitute not strength, but an encum-
brance. The supernumeraries are in the way; they not
only tumble over each other, but they aggravate the

shortages. It was so with the Confederate army in the last stages of the Civil War. The men were there; nor did the leaders want more just so long as they were unable to arm, clothe, feed and transport those they already had. Both Lee's army and Johnston's army melted away as the alternative to starvation. Under such circumstances, if all the men in the South had flocked to the colors it would only have made matters worse; the rations and ammunition would have given out so much the sooner. The artillery and commissariat trains could not be hauled when the horses were dead of inanition. In other words, after January, 1865, the possibility of organized resistance on the part of the Confederacy no longer existed. The choice lay between surrender and disbandment; or, as General Johnston subsequently wrote:—"We, without the means of purchasing supplies of any kind, or procuring or repairing arms, could continue this war only as robbers or guerillas."

The next question is,—How had this result been brought about? How did it happen that five millions of people in a country of practically unlimited extent, and one almost invulnerable to attack, were physically incapable of further organized resistance? How did they come to be so devoid of arms, food, clothing and means of transport? . . .

We are thus through elimination brought down to one factor, the blockade, as the controlling condition of Union success. In other words, that success was made possible by the undisputed naval and maritime supremacy of the North. Cut off from the outer world and all exterior sources of supply, reduced to a state of inanition by the blockade, the Confederacy was pounded to death.

Or, to put the proposition in yet another form, in the game of warfare, maritime supremacy on the part of the North—what Captain Mahan has since developed historically as the Influence of the Sea Power—even more than compensated for the military advantage of the defensive, and its interior strategic lines, enjoyed by the South. Such being the case, the greater command by one party to the conflict of men, supplies, munitions and transportation worked its natural result.

Unquestionably much could be said in support of

this contention. More than plausible, it fairly explains an outcome otherwise inexplicable now, as contrary to all foreign expectation then. . . .

19. James R. Soley: THE UNION CONTROL OF INLAND WATERS *

The total failure of the Confederate fleet on the Mississippi was largely due to bad management and to the want of a proper organization. Authority was divided between the State Government and the Confederate Government, and still further between the army, the navy, and the steamboat captains. The War and Navy Departments at Richmond did not work together. There were some differences of opinion between General Lovell, in command at New Orleans, and General Duncan, in command of the exterior defenses. Four naval officers, Rousseau, Hollins, Mitchell, and Whittle, were successively in command of the "Naval Station," a command of vague and indeterminate limits, and there were plenty of sources of disagreement between them and their colleagues of the army. They were perplexed and worried by confusing orders, and by the presence of independent agents in their own field of operations. They had no authority over the work of building the iron-clads, although constantly urged to hurry their completion. The organization of the River Defense Fleet, under Montgomery, was a direct and intentional blow at their authority, and left them without the aid of reserves whose disposition they could direct. The naval operations suffered from the lack of funds, so much so that on the 26th of February Governor Moore telegraphed to Richmond, "The Navy Department here owes nearly a million. Its credit is stopped." This condition of affairs was all the more remarkable, since the strategic position of New Orleans and the river was of vital importance to the Confederacy, and the post required above all things unity of command,—indeed, one might well say a dictatorship. Had one man of force and discretion been in

* James R. Soley, "The Union and the Confederate Navies," *Battles and Leaders of the Civil War*, Vol. I (New York, 1887), p. 628.

full command and provided with sufficient funds, the defense would at least not have presented a spectacle of complete collapse. . . .

20. Albert Bushnell Hart: THE COASTAL AND RIVER BLOCKADE *

The true military reason for the collapse of the Confederacy is to be found, not so much in the fearful hammer-like blows of Thomas, Sherman, and Grant, as in the efforts of an unseen enemy, the ships of the blockading squadrons. Never in the history of the world has a navy been called upon to perform such a difficult and almost impossible task as fell to the American Navy. A coastline of two thousand five hundred miles, with more than thirty ports practicable for blockade runners, was so sealed up that the South was thrown upon its own resources. The struggle could not be prolonged, because the army could be neither fed nor supplied from the cotton bales. The wealth of the country went to waste because it could not be exchanged for the foreign products essential for the prosecution of the war. . . .

The water-ways, both on the rivers and to the eastward, were early occupied or blockaded by the North. Union troops could be shipped from New York to Hampton Roads, or to Florida, or to Mobile, or to New Orleans; after the first months of the war no Confederate troops could be forwarded by sea. The country, therefore, was thrown upon its railroads. These roads were few, improperly built, as had been the case also in the North, and they steadily deteriorated. When the rails wore out, new ones could at last no longer be provided; when locomotives broke down, unless a Northern prisoner consented to repair them, there were often no mechanics at hand. Important links, necessary to complete the connection between the Southwest and the coast, were never built. The raids and the long marches at the end of the war so completed the ruin of the railroads that there was practically nothing left of them but the road-beds. . . .

* Albert Bushnell Hart, "Why the South Was Defeated in the Civil War," *Practical Essays on American Government* (New York, 1893), pp. 277-278.

Part VIII

STATES RIGHTS IN
THE CONFEDERACY

21. Frank Lawrence Owsley: STATES RIGHTS AND SUPPLIES *

The efforts of the states to supply their troops fall into two distinct fields: the foreign and the domestic. Let us first follow out the policy in the domestic field.

On August 1, 1862, Governor Shorter inquired of Secretary of War Randolph whether the Alabama troops had been sufficiently provided with clothing for the winter. His object, he said, in making the inquiry was "to insure a sufficient supply of clothing to the troops from this state if the state resources" would allow him to do so. On the nineteenth of November following, the legislature passed an act appropriating $250,000 for the purchase of 50,000 pairs of shoes for the Alabama troops, proposing, of course, that the Confederate government should reimburse the state for its expenditures. The war department accepted the arrangement, allowing the state to supply its troops with 50,000 pairs of shoes and a profit of $100,000 in the bargain. Alabama kept up this policy throughout the war, and by 1864 the Governor had evidently got control of the nine factories within the state and was directing their output as best served the interests of Alabama.

Governor Milton, of Florida, was very reluctantly brought into this individualistic policy. He had refused to co-operate with Governor Brown in his efforts to force the Confederate government to allow each state the unlimited right of exportation and importation, and had administered a dignified rebuke to the irrascible Brown.

* Reprinted from *State Rights in the Confederacy* by Frank Lawrence Owsley, 1925, pp. 113-122, 124-129, 149, by permission of The University of Chicago Press.

He had, it is true, during the early days of the Confederacy, sent his agents into the market to buy private arms and supplies, but as soon as the Confederacy took over the duties of supply he willingly co-operated by withdrawing his separate agents. He saw clearly the shortsightedness of each state's attempting to supply its own troops, yet before the middle of 1864, North Carolina, Georgia and Alabama having monopolized their resources, compelled him to reverse his policy and insist that the Confederate government relinquish its control of the one factory in Florida.

Georgia went in with a will to supply her troops in Confederate service. Brown, not seeing results fast enough from buying in the open market, recommended in November, 1862, that the legislature seize every factory in Georgia and control the output "till a good pair of shoes and a good suit of clothes are furnished to every (Georgia) soldier in the service who needs the assistance." The assembly approved this method, and Brown, either by force or threat, exercised practical control over the factories in Georgia whenever the necessity arose. The expenditures of the state quartermaster department may give us an idea as to the size of this business of supplying troops. In the spring of 1863 Ira J. Foster, state quartermaster, reported to Brown that he had already spent a large portion of the $1,500,000 appropriated in the fall of 1862 for supplying the Georgia soldiers. Three or four months later Brown reported to his legislature that Foster had on hand out of the proceeds of the fund 40,000 uniforms ready for distribution to Georgia troops. A large quantity, he said, had already been distributed. Feeling elated over the success of his quartermaster department, the Governor asked for an appropriation of $2,000,000 to be expended for the same purpose next year, and the legislature granted his request.

Not satisfied with buying all surplus supplies in the Georgia market, Brown sent his quartermaster into other states to compete with state and Confederate agents there. He finally got into a row with a district commander in Florida and carried his complaint to the Confederate authorities. General Lawton advised that the separate buying and the separate attempts of the states to supply their own troops was "apt to lead to competition without any material increase of the resources of the country." But he could not stop Brown as there was no legal restriction upon the state agents engaged in the collection of supplies. However, the mere objection to such a policy by the Confederate authorities did not restrain Georgia in her customary habits of clothing her own troops: Governor Brown continued his control over certain of the state's largest factories and, as we shall presently see, redoubled his efforts in blockade-running.

Finally Virginia, whose home resources had been largely under control of the Confederacy, came to the point where the policy of individual state supply seemed necessary. So the Governor, at the instance of S. Bassett French, in the summer of 1864, applied to Secretary Seddon for control of the Matoaca factory—the largest in the state. This was the last straw; Quartermaster-General Lawton literally threw up his hands and cried in despair, "et tu, Brute!" He told Seddon that "throughout the extreme Southern states one of the greatest difficulties encountered proceeded from the state executives who sought to provide for the wants of the soldiers," and who had consequently monopolized the productions of practically all the factories in their states. "These encroachments and concessions go far," he said, ". . . to defeat the object in view." He felt satisfied "that it would be better for the state authorities to allow this department to control the factory products so far as they may be needed for military purposes and abstain . . . from their auxiliary efforts to clothe the army." Now Virginia had asked to control her biggest factory. He was in despair.

However, Virginia seems to have gained control of one of her factories and later in the year the report of the Governor showed that the state had gone far on the road pointed by North Carolina and Georgia. The Governor informed the legislature that he had been engaged rather extensively in the purchase of clothing, cotton, and other supplies. He was not satisfied, though, with the matter of transportation: the Confederate government had a prior claim on the trains in the state, and he thought that Virginia should assert her rights of priority. This he recommended because in "North Carolina and other states the practice obtains . . . that whenever the governor requires a train on the road for public use, he issues his orders . . . and it is promptly furnished, to the exclusion of all other demands."

North Carolina alone succeeded in monopolizing the entire output of her factories and getting the lion's share of her other resources during the entire war. During the period before the Confederacy had organized and established its quartermaster department it had quite willingly made an agreement, in accordance with a resolution of the North Carolina legislature, to pay the commutation money over to that state and allow it to clothe its own soldiers. But in making this agreement the Confederate government had no intention of withdrawing her agents from North Carolina and turning over all the great manufacturing and natural resources to the exclusive use of that state. Yet that was exactly the manner in which North Carolina interpreted the agreement. North Carolina felt that she had met her every obligation when she supplied her own troops, and accordingly refused to contribute one yard of cloth or a single shoe, or to furnish blankets, tents, harness, and equipment of any kind to the general service during the first year of the war.

This was an unexpected turn of affairs, and the Confederate government attempted to abrogate this misinterpreted agreement in the spring of 1862. But all efforts were in vain. The state only persisted the more in its individualism. The Confederate government next proposed that all clothing and like equipment manufactured in North Carolina should be turned over to the Confederate authorities for general issue, on the condition that the troops from that state always be supplied first. But North Carolina refused to budge from her original position.

In October, 1862, the Confederacy finally abolished commutation for clothing and assumed the entire responsibility from thenceforth of clothing the troops in the Confederate service. The Confederate authorities once more attempted to persuade North Carolina to share the output of its factories with the central government, but that state was farther from it than ever, for Vance was now governor and a reactionary legislature had just been elected. The new Governor not only insisted upon monopolizing the entire output of all the factories in the state, but he insisted upon holding the Confederate government to the original agreement, to which he gave the broadest possible interpretation: he insisted that not only the factories but all other resources of North Carolina were also to be entirely devoted to her own use. Now the Confederate government, while unable to obtain any of the goods from the factories, had sent agents into North Carolina to pick up whatever they could in the open markets, and Vance, as soon as he assumed office, accused the President and the war department of violating their promises and the agreement that North Carolina should be allowed to devote all her resources to her own troops. He complained that "the country was and still is swarming with agents of the Confederate government, stripping bare our markets and putting enormous prices upon our agents." So until 1864 North Carolina continued her refusal to contribute anything to the general service in the matter of clothing, blankets, shoes, tents, harness, and such equipment. General Lawton, in January, 1864, complained bitterly that North Carolina had forty factories "from not one of which this bureau realized for years past a single yard of material for the service at large. All has been reserved . . . for North Carolina troops."

The Confederate government, in spite of the protest of Vance, continued to withdraw details. On October 5 and 8, 1864, Confederate General Orders Nos. 76 and 77 restricted details to a very narrow limit. But Governor Vance was determined to have all the men he needed if he had to withdraw the North Carolina troops from Virginia to accomplish his purpose. He sent a list of the men he wished continued on detail in his factories to General Holmes, who was commander of the department. He warned the general that "should these details . . . be unreasonably refused, I shall have to try tilts with the Confederate government." Failing to obtain all he asked for, Vance placed himself upon higher ground: he claimed "any and all persons in the actual employ of the state" as state officers, and thus obtained the exemption of his factory operatives, where before he had only had them detailed. The state legislature, by a set of resolutions, indorsed this position, and the supreme court of the state upheld it in the case of Johnson vs. Mallet. So the wheels of the North Carolina mills turned on unvexed by dependence upon Confederate detail, and North Carolina went through the war without making any contributions from her output to the general service.

More than that, North Carolina drew largely from other states. The state purchased the much-needed wool from Virginia right under the nose of the Confederate government; it bought up quantities of leather in Georgia and Florida, and even procured war material in large quantities from the trans-Mississippi department, thus still further diminishing the already meager sources for Confederate supplies. As as result of this and her blockade policy, North Carolina had on hand, while the Confederate soldiers from other states were freezing and dying from exposure, large stores of clothing and blankets. In December, 1863, North Carolina had all her troops warmly clad and had on hand—stored at Richmond, Raleigh, and other points—a surplus sufficient to meet the needs of the troops for the entire year of 1864 if the mills had not put out another yard. General Gardiner reported a vast quantity of North Carolina clothing stored in Richmond in the summer of 1864. This clothing had been there for over a year. At the time of the surrender Vance had, according to his own count, 92,000 uniforms, great stores of leather and blankets, and his troops in the field were all comfortably clad. At the same time Lee's troops were ragged and without blankets and tents.

Thus most of the Confederate states had adopted the individualistic policy of supplying their own troops, some withdrawing a part and some all of their industrial resources from the Confederate government. The consideration of a few statistics of southern resources will enable us to understand the result better. There were only 122 mills within the Confederacy in 1864. There were 9 in Alabama, 9 in South Carolina, 1 in Florida, 1 in Mississippi, 26 in Virginia, 36 in Georgia (5 of which had been wrecked) and 40 in North Carolina (well-equipped and large). Out of this total of 122 mills, the states of Virginia, Georgia, Alabama, North Carolina, and Florida were controlling 54, while the Confederate government controlled only 68, part of which were later destroyed or fell into the hands of the enemy.

The products of the foreign markets were still more

unevenly distributed than the output of the home industries, and a smaller percentage was directed toward
the common service. The seaboard states had agents in
the foreign markets floating loans and purchasing and
shipping supplies from the first. (As early as August,
1861, we hear of Georgia's representative, E. C. Anderson, making a purchase of $100,000 worth of supplies.)
North Carolina in 1861 sent John L. Payton as a special
agent to purchase supplies, and in the fall of 1862 it
sent John White and T. M. Crosson as regular commissioners, and Virginia, South Carolina, Alabama, and
Texas evidently had their representatives. These states,
after the first year and a half of the war had usually one
or two vessels with which to import and export through
the blockade, and for the rest they would have to depend upon the professional blockade runners with whom
they entered contracts or in which they bought shares.

The Confederate government had only three or four
small vessels of its own with which to run the blockade.
These could only bring in a small fraction of the materials
purchased abroad by the government, and like the states,
it too was dependent upon the professional blockade-
runners for the greater part of its import and export
trade. Thus we see that both the Confederate and state
governments were largely dependent upon the private
blockade-runners for the exportation and importation of
their supplies. The result was a cutthroat competition to
obtain control of the blockade vessels, and the corporations that owned these ships took advantage of the necessity of the Confederacy and exacted enormous profits.
They brought goods into the Confederate ports for which
they were allowed unreasonable prices, and received in
payment Confederate cotton at the rate of six cents a
pound, which they sold in Europe at twenty-four pence.
President Davis pointed out, in a message to Congress,
that six hundred bales delivered to these blockade-runners
netted the Confederate states only £6,000, while it
brought the shipowners £21,000, allowing a liberal estimate of 11 per cent loss by capture. . . .

Thus in their efforts to obtain a share in the export
and import business of the country, the states had by
their own vessels withdrawn large quantities of supplies
from the common agent, and they had by charters and

purchases of shares in private vessels often driven the
Confederacy practically out of the import business; by
fomenting strikes among the shipping companies they
had suspended the blockade-running entirely for several
weeks, and by their factiousness added immeasurably
to the already deep discontent of the masses of
people. . . .

22. Frank Lawrence Owsley: STATES RIGHTS AND CONSCRIPTION *

For the sake of clarity and continuity I shall state
briefly the chief points of contest between the states and
the Confederacy. Governor Brown, of Georgia, along
with the Stephenses and Robert Toombs, and Governor
Vance, of North Carolina, immediately entered the lists
against the policy of conscription. Their chief arguments were: conscription was unnecessary and inex-
pedient—southern men would not submit to the humiliation of being drafted, and the armies could be recruited
sufficiently by volunteering; it was unconstitutional because it would destroy the state militia; it would or could
enroll the state officers and destroy the state government;
and it would take the power of appointing military officers
out of the hands of the governor and put it in the hands
of the President. Aside from specific violations of the
Constitution, it was a violation of the spirit and tendency
of that instrument because it placed too much power in
the hands of President Davis. Brown and Vance were
the leaders, in their respective states, of the opposition
during the early years of conscription, and were the only
real opponents among the state governors up until the
law of February 17, 1864, which had for its aim the
transfer of all the effective state troops to the Confederate reserves. After that law was passed practically every
state arrayed itself against the central government on
the conscription question. Brown and Vance became
more obstreperous than ever, while governors such as
Milton, of Florida, and Clark, of Mississippi, "kept their

* Reprinted from *State Rights in the Confederacy* by Frank
    Lawrence Owsley, 1925, pp. 203-215, by permission of
    The University of Chicago Press.

mouths shut and sawed wood" and rendered as much damage as their more noisy neighbors.

In the controversy over conscription—aside from general obstruction—the states asserted several claims with great success and corresponding hurt to the Confederacy: the exemption of state officers, militia officers, and state troops. So much for the main points of the narrative. It will be our chief task to point out in detail the numbers actually withdrawn by this wholesale exemption policy of the states. . . .

Governor Brown claimed successfully almost all the state officers—he exempted clerks, deputy clerks, sheriffs, deputy sheriffs, and their deputies, magistrates, notary publics, tax collectors, deputy collectors, and their clerks, judges—in fact Brown exempted any man whom he wished to by attaching him to some shadowy and elusive official position. Even the employees on the state and public railways and factories fell into the category of "state officer." Then he turned to his militia and granted every member a commission who was not already exempt by virtue of being a state officer or on account of physical disability. It was a common saying that "every private in Joe Brown's militia holds an officer's commission," and this was just about true, for it was pointed out time after time that there were about 3,000 militia officers between the ages of eighteen and forty-five in Brown's militia. Colonel Browne (of the Confederate service) reported 2,751 in November, 1864, as being subject to general service. General Howell Cobb, who was in position to know, placed the number at not less than 3,000 men of military age. The number of men exempted as state or militia officers ranged from 8,000 to 15,000. Colonel Browne reported the number on November 29, 1864, as 5,478 civil officers and 2,751 militia officers. General Cobb about this time estimated the number at over 6,000 county and militia officers, exclusive of state officers and operatives in the factories. President Davis gave the number of able-bodied men in *Georgia* who were classed as "officers" as 15,000. It is probable that the figures were something more than 8,000 and that Davis was approximately correct, for the numbers reported by Cobb and Colonel Browne were those obtained through the conscription office, which only showed those who had presented their certificates of exemption to the conscription officers. This did not cover anything like the whole body of exempts, as Brown, claiming that a blanket proclamation exempted all officers named therein, never issued a certificate to an officer until that officer was cornered by the Confederate authorities. As Preston said, the 8,000 reported was only "progressive" and that as time passed more exempts would show up.

These facts lend much color to the statement of the enrolling officer in Georgia to General Cobb that there were more men, during 1864, between eighteen and forty-five staying at home than had gone from the state into Confederate service during the war.

In *Mississippi,* during 1864 and 1865, the situation became as bad as in Georgia. Governor Clark quietly asserted his rights to all state and militia officers and refused to be drawn into any controversy. The Governor insisted that his proclamation served as a blanket exemption for the classes of officers mentioned therein, and that no personal certificate from him should be given. Acting on this principle he actually granted only about 200 certificates, which caused the conscription officers to report only that number of officers exempted in Mississippi, when as a matter of fact he had exempted several thousand men of military age. Brigadier General H. W. Walter, who made an inspection tour through Mississippi in November, 1864, complained of the fact that the bureau reports showed only 204 state exempts when as a matter of common knowledge there were over 2,300 county, and nearly 2,000 state officers exempted under the Governor's proclamation. "This abuse is greater in Georgia," said General Walter, but, he protested, "that state shows in the conscript reports the truth, however discreditable. Mississippi enjoys the benefits but avoids the stigma." These numbers do not include the militia officers who must have numbered not less than 2,000, since, as we have seen in the chapter on local defense, there were several thousand state militia in active service. These figures for Mississippi throw a light upon the reports of the conscript bureau, which Preston always admitted were "progressive" and not final. It means that most of his reports of exempts are under the actual number exempted.

General Walter drew a similar picture for Alabama.

The official figures for Alabama, 1,333, were much higher
than for Mississippi in 1864, which showed that the Governor had exacted his pound of flesh in 1863, as it took
several months to get these figures. As in the case of
Mississippi, the numbers reported were meaningless, for
the governor in 1864 claimed every civil and military
officer in the state, from the police in Selma to the governor in Montgomery, making several thousands rather
than a few hundred.

Governor Smith, of Virginia, remained friendly to the
Confederate policy, but not so his legislature. That body
by 1864 insisted that every officer named in the constitution and laws of the state was essential to the dignity and
sovereignty—and we might add, happiness—of the state.
Smith delivered the legislature an indignant lecture for
having exempted the great host of state and county officers named in the constitution and laws of the state,
especially the 2,000 magistrates whose counties were
within the enemies' lines, thus rendering them without
official duties. The total number of officers thus exempted
is not shown on the records, but we gather an idea that
there were several thousand from the fact that there were,
as already stated, 2,000 justices of the peace from the
invaded counties alone. Governor Smith said that the
officers from these counties were enough by themselves
"to turn the tide of a great battle."

Up until the late fall of 1864 South Carolina had asserted no claims over her state officers when the Confederate government required them for military service.
As Governor Bonham wrote Governor Vance September
28, 1864, no persons were "reserved to the state, but all
have gone into the Confederate service, from the classes
of militia officers, magistrates, deputy clerks, and deputy
sheriffs" on up to the highest officers of the state. But
even when Bonham wrote this letter to Vance *South Carolina* was reaching the breaking-point, and in December
the legislature virtually repudiated all obligations to the
Confederate government. This legislature nullified the
slave impressment act of the Confederate government and
then passed an exemption act that, according to General
Preston of the Bureau of Conscription, would have "the
effect to nullify the existing law of Congress and forestall
any further legislation of Congress looking to citizens of

South Carolina for an increase of the army." At one stroke South Carolina went to the front ranks of the opposition.

In order to understand just where *South Carolina* stood, it will benefit us to examine the provisions of this law. The governor could claim the exemption from Confederate military service of the members of the legislature, all judges of courts of law and equity, attorney- and solicitor-generals, secretaries of state, comptroller-general, state auditor and two assistants, treasurers of the upper and lower divisions, adjutant and inspector general and one assistant, quarter-master general, commissary general, state engineer and one assistant, aides-de-camp to the governor for each brigade, private secretary for the governor and his clerks, sheriffs and clerks of the courts, registers and commissioners in equity, tax collectors, cashiers, bookkeepers, and one teller of the state bank and each of its branches, cadets of the military academy, teachers in South Carolina College, superintendent, physicians, and keepers of the lunatic asylum, members of the Board of Relief of Soldiers' Families, the president, cashier, bookkepeers, and one teller for each bank and savings institution, deputy sheriffs, one editor for each newspaper and such pressmen and printers as the editor might need, all members of police and fire departments at Columbia and Charleston, all employees in factories and public works belonging to the state, all college teachers, and any number of white persons the governor might think necessary for policing the country. The Governor executed this law to the letter. During the last few months of the Confederacy, when the state-rights reaction held sway, the Governor probably exempted several thousand able-bodied men from military service.

The records do not tell us all about *Texas,* but we will remember that in our study of local defense the legislature claimed all conscripts not in Confederate service at the time, and that Murrah detailed 5,000 men to haul cotton for the state. Again, we will remember that General Greer complained to the Confederate authorities that every officer, down to the lowest deputies and subdeputies, were exempted by the state judges through the writ of habeas corpus.

But, as in some other state-rights claims, *North Caro-*

lina was easily first in the number of so-called state officers exempted. Vance had kept as many men for local defense as possible and he did likewise in the matter of state and militia officers. He had asserted this claim soon after coming into office, laying claim to the pettiest officials imaginable as being necessary for the efficient governing of the state. By 1864 Vance was making a much wider claim to exemptions: when the Confederate government attempted to withdraw the details from the forty North Carolina factories working for Vance, or refused to grant new details in order to force these factories to turn over part of their output to the Confederacy, he coolly claimed every operative he needed on the ground that he was a state officer. Vance boldly announced to the Confederate authorities that beside the state officers heretofore claimed, he claimed "any and all persons in the actual employ of the state in any department where the law enjoins duties to be done which require the employment of such persons." Shortly after this, Preston, of the conscript bureau, reported that the Governor had exempted "all persons employed in any form by the state . . . such as workmen in factories, salt markets, etc.," and that the bureau no longer had the power to enforce the law "in opposition to the Governor's certificate or claims." . . .

23. Frank Lawrence Owsley: STATES RIGHTS: GENERAL OBSERVATIONS *

The idea of state rights and local patriotism resulted in each of the Confederate states undertaking its own local defense, aside from the general defense of the Confederacy. In 1861 this resulted in a shortage of arms and munitions for the general service. The Confederate government had at the outset about 190,000 small arms and about 8,000 cannon, while the states had about 350,000 small arms in addition to the large stock in private hands. In their desire to protect themselves, the states failed to pool all these arms for the general service but kept many

* Reprinted from *State Rights in the Confederacy* by Frank Lawrence Owsley, 1925, pp. 272-277, by permission of The University of Chicago Press.

of them in their arsenals or placed them in the hands of the local state troops. The result was that about 200,000 volunteers for Confederate service were rejected the first year of the war because the government could not arm them. The reports of Secretaries of War Walker and Benjamin substantiate these figures. This means that if the states had surrendered their arms freely the Confederacy would, with the aid of imported and captured munitions, have put 600,000 instead of 400,000 men in the field the first year.

After 1861 it became more a question of men than arms. Arms a plenty were available to equip 600,000 men. But by this time the states had placed in local organizations most of the surplus man-power willing to fight. It is probable that over 100,000 men were thus held in state service in the spring of 1862. These troops were very poor as a rule, not being subject to discipline of a very rigorous kind. We might say that these 100,000 men were virtually lost to military service, judged in the light of what they actually contributed toward the war.

Conscription in 1862 disbanded many of these. Many were, however, retained, especially by South Carolina and North Carolina, on the grounds that they were "troops of war" and not militia. Soon after this, in spite of the law of conscription, the states which had lost their troops began to rebuild the old organizations. They did so usually with the consent of the Confederate government; but this consent was given reluctantly and under political duress. Conscript material composed nine-tenths of these forces. Finally it was determined by the Confederate government to gain control of the state organizations—those above forty-five and between sixteen and seventeen—for local defense under Confederate authority, while those between eighteen and forty-five should be transferred for general service. The conscript law of 1864 attempted this. It failed. The governors, most of them, kept their troops, under the right of keeping "troops of war." Some gave them up, but only when the war had about come to an end.

Thus we see that from a military point of view this local-defense policy did incalculable damage. But this was not all: the attempt of the Confederacy to obtain control of these troops resulted in many bitter quarrels between the Confederate and state authorities, which helped greatly to destroy that spirit of co-operation so essential to a government like the Confederacy.

Not only did the states maintain their own military establishments, but they exercised a considerable control over their troops in Confederate service. Brown and Vance, especially, considered that all Confederate troops were, in reality, militia, and that they had the constitutional right to appoint officers to fill vacancies among these troops.

The states during the first year of the war objected to direct volunteering. They demanded that the troops be raised through, and submitted by, state agency to the Confederate government.

Most important of all was the attempt of each state to supply its troops in Confederate service. By the end of the war the states were controlling 60 out of 122 cotton factories for this purpose, leaving only 62 for Confederate use. North Carolina had 40 cotton mills and did not allow the Confederate government a yard of cloth from them for any except North Carolina troops during the entire war.

The foreign source of supply also experienced this same competition between the states and the Confederacy. Each state did a blockade business wherever possible and, to that extent, withdrew supplies from general distribution, because only a limited amount could run the blockade, and the more the states got the less the Confederacy got. Davis tried to stop this attempt of the states to supply their troops in the Confederate service. He and Secretary of War Seddon both pointed out time after time that this . . . would create jealousy and discontent in the army and friction between Confederate and state agents. The protests were of no avail. The state-rights party insisted on this individualistic policy in the face of all attempts of the Confederacy to assert itself in this business. The results of this policy may be seen in the case of North Carolina. Governor Vance boasted that at the end of the war he had every one of his soldiers well clothed and had on hand in warehouses 92,000 uniforms, thousands of blankets, shoes, and tents. But at the same time Lee's men in Virginia were barefooted, almost without blankets, tents, and clothing. Vance had enough uniforms to give every man in Lee's army two apiece. . . .

Part IX

INTERNAL DISSENSION IN
THE CONFEDERACY

24. Georgia Lee Tatum: DISLOYALTY AND DESERTION *

In view of the bitter opposition to secession and the strong Union sentiment existing in Northwest Arkansas, it is not surprising to find the Unionists organizing not only against the Confederacy but also for self-protection. While the question of secession was being considered, both the secessionists and unionists had tried to create public sentiment in their favor, and after the war began they continued their efforts. The Germans and the Irish never showed any inclination to enlist in the Confederate army. The secessionists attempted to rally the people to the support of the Confederacy by declaring that its failure would bring Negro equality, which would inevitably result in trouble with the Negroes. This statement took an increased significance in June, 1861, when a plot was unearthed among the Negroes in Monroe County to murder all the white men and, in case they offered any resistance, the women and children. Several Negroes were arrested on the charge of attempting to start this insurrection, and three—two men and one girl—were hanged. Although the fear of Negro equality caused some of the more ignorant to rally to the support of the Confederacy, the better educated natives and the foreign-born Irish and Germans were not disturbed by this prediction and continued to refuse to give their support. . . .

By 1863 the dissatisfaction had increased, and the

* Georgia Lee Tatum, *Disloyalty in the Confederacy* (Chapel Hill: University of North Carolina Press, 1934), pp. 38, 42-43, 60, 63, 64-65, 69-70, 77-79, 107-108, 112-114, 117, 125, 127, 150-151, 154-155. Reprinted by permission.

presence of the Federals in the state made the disloyal very bold. Large numbers of men deserted to the enemy. By July only one Confederate newspaper remained in the state. By December eight regiments, consisting of both whites and blacks, had enlisted in the Federal service. Life and property, especially in North Arkansas, were insecure, and Union sympathizers fled to the Union army for protection while the Confederate sympathizers went south. By the fall of 1863 the Federals had captured Little Rock and had cleared the country northeast of the Arkansas River of organized Confederate soldiers—an accomplishment which encouraged many to advocate publicly a return to the Union. . . .

After the reverses of the Confederacy in 1863 the enthusiasm of the people for the Confederacy very perceptibly declined, because many believed the South could not win and dreaded the further sacrifices of war. As a result, not only the disloyal but many of the loyal began to urge peace. Men refused to go into service, and desertions from the army increased. On July 28, 1863, General Pillow reported that he believed there were between 8,000 and 10,000 "deserters and tory conscripts in the mountains of [North] Alabama, many of whom have deserted the second, third, and (some of them) the fourth time." As fast as they were caught and sent back to the Army of the Tennessee, they promptly deserted and not only brought their arms with them but also stole from their comrades all the ammunition that they could take away. Many of their bands were strong enough to drive away the small bodies of cavalry which were sent to arrest them. Several officers sent out to bring them in were killed. When too hard pressed by the Confederate forces sent after them, they ran "into the enemy's lines to elude capture." Pillow requested that when captured they be sent to the Army of Virginia, from which they would find it more difficult to return home. . . .

As before noted, general disaffection and the organization known as the Peace Society were not confined to North Alabama. In the early part of January, 1863, soldiers had to be used to suppress "Unionism and treason" in Henry County, in the southeastern corner of the state. About this time the Federals raided Coffee County. In order to clear out the deserters, tories, and runaway

Negroes from Southeast Alabama and West Florida, Governor Shorter gave J. H. Clanton the authority to enroll men for the defense of that section. Believing it necessary for defense and hoping many who were hiding to evade the conscript law would come home and enlist to defend their homes and families, the Governor authorized Clanton to enroll conscripts in Coffee, Covington, Dale, Pike, Henry, and Barbour counties, as well as those not subject to the conscription law. Some of the conscripts came out of hiding and joined Clanton's brigade, but many refused and the disloyal continued to cause trouble. In August Governor Shorter had to appeal to General Howell Cobb for aid in suppressing a band of deserters and conscripts who had for some time been infesting the lower part of Henry County, Alabama, and West Florida. They were in such numbers as to alarm the loyal citizens, against whom they were making threats of personal injury. A small force of state guards captured six or seven men liable for Confederate service and started them back under escort for safe-keeping; but a superior force in ambush attacked them, freed the prisoners, and killed one of the escorts. Cobb, who was already aware of the disaffection in that section, agreed that it was dangerous and asked for military authority to deal with the traitors. Since the men were generally not guilty of an overt act, it was useless to turn them over to a civil court, because they would be released.

In December, 1863, the Peace Society was discovered among the men of General Clanton's brigade, which was stationed at Pollard in Conecuh County. Just before Christmas between sixty and seventy of his soldiers mutinied and the whole scheme, which was to lay down their arms on Christmas day and go home, was exposed. Many of these men were from the poorer classes of Southeast Alabama and had suffered much during the war. They had never seen service and, being stationed near their homes, were under home influence. Some of them were exempts who had entered service because Clanton was a popular leader and they feared they might be forced into the army under someone else later. Others were substitutes and conscripts who had little patriotism and had been forced into the army or had responded to the Governor's call to come home to protect their families. Besides these, there were a few veteran soldiers. Being encouraged by people of their own section who were members of the Peace Society and having among their number some members of a secret organization—probably the Order of the Heroes of America—a number of the dissatisfied in Clanton's brigade had formed a peace society "with all the usual accompaniment of signs, passwords, grips, oaths, and obligations." They had bound themselves together "by solemn oaths never to fight the enemy, to desert, and to encourage desertion," and to do anything else that would aid in breaking down the Confederate government and ending the war. Seventy of the men who were members of the society were immediately arrested and sent to Mobile for trial by court-martial. In January, 1864, Clanton had many more arrested. After he had made an effort to purge his regiment of those he thought would cause trouble, he, Governor Watts, and others begged for another chance for the remainder of his regiment. Bolling Hall's battalion, which had been sent to the Western army because it had such a peace society in it, they said, had made a brilliant record at Chickamauga and in other battles. After the Battle of Chickamauga, its colors showed eighty-two bullet holes. Clanton believed his men would prove just as true to their colors if given a chance to fight. He insisted that the society had not originated among them but had been brought in by men from Hilliard's legion and Gracie's brigade and that but few of his men had joined it for treasonable purposes. Watts was anxious to have them sent to North Alabama, where they were badly needed. Colonel Swanson, of the Fifty-ninth and Sixty-first Alabama Regiments (consolidated), who investigated Clanton's men, said there seemed to be no leaders nor any general materialized plan on the part of the men; but that it seemed to be the general disposition on the part of substitutes, foreigners, and the poorer classes to accept terms and end the war. These people said that since they had nothing, there was nothing for them to fight for. . . .

By the fall of 1864, besides the conscripts and deserters from Alabama, there were many deserters from the commands in other states hiding in the mountains of North Alabama. After the fall of Atlanta the number of stragglers and deserters greatly increased, and it was estimated that six thousand of them were in the state—

some in every county. Near the close of the year several thousand of Hood's army went over to the enemy and took the oath of allegiance to the United States or scattered to their homes. In many counties of Alabama, bordering on Florida, Georgia, and Mississippi, armed bands of deserters and tory citizens prevented the conscription officers from enforcing their orders. Loyal citizens, especially in North and Southeast Alabama, suffered considerably from the disloyal. Without question, some who deserted at this time were influenced by the Peace Society, although, no doubt, many men went home to protect their families from the outlaws and many others went because they felt it was useless to continue the war.

In the winter of 1864-65 General P. D. Roddy and several other Confederate officers were carrying on treasonable negotiations for peace with the Federal authorities. J. J. Giers, a brother-in-law of State Senator Patton, was in constant communication with Grant. In one of his reports to Grant, he said that Major McGaughey, Roddy's brother-in-law, had been sent by Roddy and another Confederate general to meet Giers near Moulton in Lawrence County to find out what terms could be obtained for Alabama. Major McGaughey told Giers that the people of Alabama considered that affairs were hopeless and wanted peace; and that if the terms were acceptable, steps would be taken to induce Governor Watts to accept them. In case the Governor refused the terms, a civil and military movement which would include three-fourths of the state would be begun to organize a state government. All of the leading men, McGaughey said, indorsed the plan, and all of the counties north of the cotton belt and those in the southeastern part of the state were ready to return to the Union. The peace leaders wanted the Washington administration to announce at once a policy of gradual emancipation in order to reassure those afraid of outright abolition of slavery; and to "disintegrate the rebel soldiery" of North Alabama, which, they said, had never been strongly devoted to the Confederacy. . . .

In 1864 the outlook was gloomy; the hearts of many failed, and the disaffection increased. When Sherman came into the state, many were glad to submit to any terms to prevent the devastation of the country. The disloyal were greatly encouraged in their work because of the disaffection shown by Governor Brown and Vice-President Stephens. While Davis was with Hood's army at Atlanta and in other places in Georgia, trying to rally the people to the cause, Governor Brown and Vice-President Stephens, who had not been in Richmond for nearly two years, were doing what they could to break down the influence of the Davis administration. When Davis called on the Georgia militia to aid in expelling Sherman from the state, Governor Brown treated his call with contempt and demanded that the Georgians who were with Lee be returned to do the fighting. No man in the state openly showed more disaffection than the Governor. The day Davis closed his campaign of encouragement, Stephens, in Augusta, told the people "that the resources of the South were exhausted and that peace ought to be made." He even talked of entering into a compact with the Northern Democracy to control the policy of the Union. Peace meetings were held and many were clamoring for a convention of all the states in which the differences between the North and South might be settled and the war ended. Soldiers continued to show disaffection. A large number of the Georgia troops stationed at Dalton said openly they would lay down their arms and refuse to fight any longer if they were ordered to move from Dalton.

When Sherman started on his march across the state, the demand for peace increased. While he was in Savannah, a secret meeting of the disloyal in Tatnall and Liberty counties was held, at which resolutions were adopted and forwarded to Sherman. The resolutions stated that the undersigned citizens of Liberty and Tatnall counties were either deserters from the so-called army of the Confederate States or men above the conscription age who would never aid in the rebellion; that they would band together under the leadership of some suitable person to protect themselves against the rebels; that the occupation of Georgia by the Federals met their approval and they would render any service asked by the Federals; that they had opposed secession and regarded its supporters as traitors. Death was to be the penalty for anyone revealing any of the proceedings of the meetings or any of the obligations of the members of their band.

Sherman replied to these people that he would do all in his power to encourage and defend them in their course; that if they would remain at home quietly, and call back their sons and neighbors from the army, he would furnish them ammunition to protect themselves and their property; that if the rebels did them any harm, he would retaliate; and that their produce would be protected when sent to market. In order that the Federals might be able to distinguish these men from the loyal Confederates when they brought their produce to Savannah, Sherman advised them to form a league and adopt some common certificate.

Disaffection increased in the state, and the disloyal continued to give aid to the Federals. Lieutenant John L. West, First Florida Infantry of the Confederate army, who left his regiment on February 15, 1864, at Dalton, Georgia, reported to the Federals that Jos. E. Johnston had between thirty thousand and thirty-five thousand men; that he did not "intend to give battle at Dalton, but [would] withdraw toward Atlanta if pressed by Grant"; that the men had no shoes; that their rations consisted of Florida beef, which they could not eat, and of corn; that "the spirit of the army was in favor of peace. The men re-enlist only to get furloughs and never return." The demand for peace and the disaffection continued in Georgia until the war closed. . . .

During the war there was much disaffection in North Carolina. The Order of the Heroes of America became widespread there and was in constant communication with the North. Because of a red string worn in the lapel of the coat, in allusion to the Bible story of Rahab, the order was commonly known as the "Red Strings" or the "Red String Band." Although the Order of the Heroes of America may not have been organized until some time after the war began, disaffection and active opposition appeared in North Carolina the first year of the war and increased alarmingly as the struggle continued. As early as September, 1861, Rush C. Hawkins, commander of the Federal troops at Fort Clark, Hatteras Inlet, reported that "one-third of the State of North Carolina would be back in the Union within two weeks" if the United States forces were near enough to protect the people. This was no doubt an exaggeration, though the loyalty to the Union, manifested when Hatteras was captured, is proof that not all of the people could be depended upon to support the Confederacy.

Disaffection was far from being confined to any one section of the state, but its first manifestation was in the East. As soon as the Federals captured the forts on the eastern coast, the citizens of Hatteras petitioned the Union commander at Hatteras Inlet not to treat them as rebels, since they had neither taken up arms against the Union nor voted to withdraw from it. Within a week, more than two hundred and fifty had taken the oath of allegiance to the United States and had promised to keep the Federals informed of the movements of the Confederates, in return for protection by the Federal army. Secret meetings of the disloyal were held in the counties bordering Pamlico Sound, and many acted as spies for the enemy. Hyde, Washington, Tyrrell, and Beaufort counties showed so much disaffection that the loyal Conferedate citizens became alarmed. Many of the loyal men had volunteered, while all of the unionists and those that were lukewarm remained at home. Moreover, many felt that since they were already in the hands of the Federals, submission was their only course. . . .

The bitter party spirit which developed during 1862 increased the dissatisfaction and disloyalty. Holden and others led an opposition to the Governor, whose policy was "the last man and the last dollar" if necessary to win the war, a policy which did not augur well for those who did not wish to fight and who were working for peace. Holden attacked both the state and the Confederate administrations. Not only did he continue to harp on "a rich man's war and a poor man's fight," but he also brought the charge that the war was being conducted as a "party war," that only strong secessionists and Democrats were allowed to hold office in either the state or the Confederate administration; and he urged that "peace men" be elected to both state and Confederate offices in the August elections. Although Holden advocated Zebulon Vance, who was referred to in the North as the "Northern or Federal candidate," for governor, many believed Holden was paving the way for his own candidacy. Jonathan Worth and Josiah Turner, who opposed the war and were then demanding peace, joined Holden and his followers in supporting Vance for governor against William Johnston, the pro-Davis and Confederate man, who stood for an "unremitting prosecution of the war" and for "no compromise with enemies, traitors, or tories."

The agitation of Holden and his followers soon began to bear fruit. By March, 1862, there were so many deserters in Chatham County that a company had to be sent there to arrest them. But since the criminal code in North Carolina made no provision for the punishment of deserters, it was difficult to do anything with them when caught. Many of the citizens asked that a military court be established in western North Carolina to deal with the disloyal, but this was not done. The statement was constantly made that extreme disloyalty existed in Davidson, Forsyth, Randolph, and Guilford counties. In these counties there was a large Quaker element that opposed the war, not so much because of their objection to the Confederacy as because of their religious beliefs. Some of the men volunteered, but many refused to fight. Deserters, knowing of the sentiment against war in these counties, collected in them in great numbers. Conditions in other counties also caused alarm. In Yadkin and Wilkes the deserters threatened to interfere with the coming elections, and troops were sent to prevent it. In Madison County and farther west, General E. Kirby Smith felt it necessary to send troops to deal with the deserters.

When the election was held, the small vote for Johnston and the "tone and temper of many of the men elected to the General Assembly" indicated the strength of the "peace party" and proved that the enthusiasm for the Confederacy was waning. Vance defeated Johnston almost two to one in the army. In Chatham, Guilford, Randolph, Forsyth, Yadkin, Iredell, and Wilkes counties, where disaffection was prevalent and deserters had collected, Vance received about twenty times as many votes as Johnston. In forty-three of the counties of the state, Vance's majority was more than 19,000.

The policy of Governor Vance and other state officials, in obtaining the release of men accused of disloyalty, gave much aid and encouragement to the disaffected.

In December the General Assembly instructed the Governor to demand that Davis return a preacher of Orange County who had been arrested as a spy by the Confederate authorities and imprisoned in Richmond. Not only did they secure the release of this man (against whom the Confederate authorities had found no evidence), but, by the use of the writ of habeas corpus, they also released many North Carolinians who were imprisoned at Salisbury on the charge of disloyalty. Chief Justice Pearson believed that the conscription law was unconstitutional and from this time until the close of the war, there seems to be no record of his having refused a writ of habeas corpus to secure the release of conscripts, deserters, or anyone accused of disloyalty. . . .

Disloyalty in the army was so great that the Confederate officers became alarmed. On April 18, 1863, General Lee informed Secretary of War Seddon that there had been "frequent desertions from the North Carolina regiments." Some of the deserters were going home, but the enemy claimed that many were coming to them and giving information. At that time, Lee held six disloyal North Carolinians who had been captured by General D. H. Hill and sent to him. The three that were of conscription age, Lee assigned to North Carolina regiments; but he advised Seddon to send them into the interior, since they would be not only worthless in his army but dangerous. Lee was quite sure they would desert from his own army in Northern Virginia within a week and would carry to the enemy the information that they had collected in North Carolina, Richmond, and elsewhere, as well as any facts concerning the intended movement of his army which they had chanced to hear. The three men over conscription age were sent back to North Carolina with charges against them; but, no doubt, they were released as many others had been. . . .

In central and western North Carolina, the disloyal were organizing into bands of from fifty up to several hundred. In Cherokee County, they captured and assumed a form of military occupation of a town; in Wilkes, five hundred organized into a regiment, intrenched themselves in a camp, and drilled regularly; in Randolph, between three and four hundred organized for resistance. There were also large numbers in Yadkin, Iredell, and

Catawba counties. Lieutenant George Lay said that these bands "are not only determined to kill in avoiding apprehension (having just put to death yet another of our enrolling officers), but their esprit de corps extends to killing in revenge as well as in prevention of the capture of each other. So far they seem to have had no trouble for subsistence. While the disaffected feed them from sympathy, the loyal do so from fear." Living up to their obligations in the Order of the Heroes of America, these bands, too, sent letters to the army to get men to desert, and to promise protection to all who would join them.

When the congressional election took place in the fall of 1863, eight of the ten members chosen for the Confederate Congress were "reported to be in favor of peace." George W. Logan, who represented the Tenth District, had been nominated in one of Holden's peace meetings. . . .

By the close of 1863, discontent and peace sentiment had become so generally diffused among the people of North Carolina that Vance informed Davis that the discontent could be removed only by an attempt to negotiate with the North, to which Davis replied that it could not be done because of the refusal of the Lincoln government.

By 1864 there were so many deserters in West North Carolina that there was no stigma attached to desertion; and because of the warm welcome accorded them and the safety assured them, deserters not only from North Carolina but from practically every state in the Confederacy, lurked in the mountains and plundered, murdered, or drove out the loyal citizens as they pleased. . . .

Since the Confederate government in Tennessee collapsed in 1862, the unionists and others who were not in sympathy with the Confederacy found it comparatively easy, from that time on, to give aid to the Union and to work against the Confederacy.

When the first conscription law was passed, there was such an exodus of the unionists to the mountains of East Tennessee and the neighboring states that men known as guides or "pilots" spent their time in conducting parties of refugees through the woods and mountains to places of safety, or to the Federal army if they wished to fight. Captain Daniel Ellis, one of the most noted of this class, claims that he piloted ten thousand men to the Federal army in Kentucky and Tennessee. This, however, is probably an exaggeration. Other famous "pilots" were Spencer Deaton, Seth Lea, and Frank Hodge, of Knox County; Isaac Bolinger, of Campbell; Washington Vann and William B. Reynolds, of Anderson; and James Lane, of Greene. All of these conducted many parties to Kentucky. Captain William B. Reynolds, and no doubt many others, acted as pilot, spy, recruiting officer, and fighter for the Federals, as the occasion demanded. "He would slip into Knoxville, bringing messages and news [to the Federals and to the unionists there], then, ascertaining all that was important about the Confederate army, would slip out and return to Kentucky, leading back a small number of recruits or refugees."

These guides received much valuable assistance from women who collected information for them and for the Federals. One of the most widely known was Mrs. Jeannette Laurimer Mabry, the wife of Colonel George W. Mabry, of Knox County. Although her husband and his family were loyal Confederates, she refused to ally herself with the cause of the South. "She always had the latest news from the front" and was in communication with practically every guide and envoy from the Federal lines.

Not only were East Tennesseans outside of the army loyal to the Union and in constant communication with the Federals, but many in Confederate service were disloyal to the Confederacy. On March 15, 1862, General E. Kirby Smith reported to General Cooper that the soldiers from East Tennessee could not be relied upon to do picket duty; that some of the officers were suspected of being disloyal; and that he believed some of the East Tennessee regiments were disloyal. . . .

Many soldiers were leaving the Confederate army during the fall of 1863 and going over to the enemy. General Rosecrans reported, in September, that under the authority he had previously received, he had organized and mustered into service for twelve months several companies of loyal Alabamans, and that many more deserters were asking for permission to enlist with him.

The deserters reported great dissatisfaction among the Confederate troops from Tennessee, Alabama, and North Georgia. In East Tennessee, opposition to the Confederacy continued to increase until the close of the war.

The damage done to the Confederate cause by the unionists in East Tennessee was considerable. The records show that thirty-one thousand Tennesseans enlisted in the Union army, and Temple and others say there were about four thousand others who fought against the Confederacy. Had these gone into the Confederate army, they would not only have increased the Confederate forces by this number but also have decreased the Federal forces by the same amount. And further, in addition to the loss of the large number of men who enlisted in the Federal army and fought against the Confederacy, from five to ten thousand Confederate soldiers are said to have been required to hold in check the unionists left at home in East Tennessee. Therefore, it is clear that, had these Tennesseans adhered to the Confederate cause, the numbers in the Confederate army would have been increased considerably. Although the direct positive influence of these Union soldiers furnished by Tennessee cannot be estimated exactly in terms of the winning of battles, it seems certain that it was important. Moreover, one cannot estimate the value of the information and other aid given to the Federals by the unionists. Beyond question, the number of desertions not only from Tennessee but also from other states influenced by Tennessee, and the moral support which East Tennesseans gave to Lincoln and the North by showing that almost in the heart of the Confederacy there was a large compact body of men who defied the Confederacy and espoused the cause of the Union, helped to sustain the morale of the Federals and to weaken the morale of the Confederates. . . .

25. Bell Irvin Wiley: INTERNAL DISSENSION IN THE CONFEDERACY *

Perhaps the most costly of the Confederacy's short-comings was the disharmony among its people. A cursory glance at the Confederacy reveals numerous instances of bitter strife, and one who delves deeply into the literature of the period may easily conclude that Southerners hated each other more than they did the Yankees. Behind the battle of bullets waged with the invaders was an enormous war of words and emotions among Confederates themselves which began before secession and which eventually became so intense that it sapped the South's vitality and hastened Northern victory.

One of the most notorious instances of disharmony was that of the President and Vice-President. Davis and Stephens got along amicably in the early days of the Confederacy but differences in political background and the fact that both were sickly, stubborn and sensitive, worked against continuing cordiality. Stephens chafed under the inactivity inherent in his position and when Davis in the autumn of 1861 ceased turning frequently to him for counsel a coolness developed between them. Using ill health as an excuse, Stephens in 1862 spent about half of his time in Georgia. Before the end of 1862 he was denouncing conscription and other major acts of the administrative program. In 1863 he virtually abandoned the vice-presidency and launched an open attack on Davis and his policies. His antagonism increased with the passing of time and in 1864 he teamed up with his brother, Linton Stephens, and Governor Joseph E. Brown of Georgia in an all-out effort to discredit Davis and his conduct of the government and initiate steps looking to peace and reunion. In March, 1864, the Confederacy was treated to the spectacle of its Vice-President castigating the President and the administration in a three hour speech before the Georgia Legislature.

Principle entered to some extent into the disagreement between Davis and Stephens, as the Vice-President insisted that the sovereignty of the state should always be

* Bell Irvin Wiley, *The Road to Appomattox* (Memphis: Memphis State College Press, 1956), pp. 78-84, 85-90, 91, 94-96, 99-102. Reprinted by permission.

preeminent while Davis believed that at least during the war both states and individuals should yield to the central government some of their accustomed rights. But Professor James Z. Rabun, who has made a careful study of the war-time relations of Stephens and Davis, attributes their quarrel primarily to pettiness, jealousy and blindness on the part of the Vice-President. It is possible that Davis could have prevented the break by playing to Stephens's vanity and making him a more active partner in the administration, but flattery was not among the President's talents. And Stephens could never have been enthusiastic about a secondary role. The Vice-President's course would have been more admirable if he had resigned in 1862. For him to stay in the administration and openly fight it was as unbecoming to the man as it was hurtful to the Southern cause.

Relations between Davis and his cabinet appeared relatively harmonious, but beneath the smooth surface considerable tension existed. Significant of the smouldering dissatisfaction was the fact that Davis made eight changes in a cabinet of six members, and four of these were in the war office. In contrast, Lincoln made only five changes in his official family of seven members. Only two of Davis's cabinet members, Mallory and Reagan, held their posts throughout the war, and if Davis had known what Mallory was writing in his diary about the conduct of the government he would probably have given the navy another head before the war was a year old.

Benjamin was the only cabinet member with whom Davis maintained a warm and close relationship, and the cordiality was due in no small part to Benjamin's adeptness at flattery. Most of the others chafed at the seeming unimportance of their positions and some resented the President's failure to take them more fully into his confidence. Randolph, as previously noted, left the cabinet in a huff, and Toombs and Hunter both became bitter opponents of Davis after their resignations.

Davis's difficulties with the cabinet were as nothing in comparison with the dissension between the President and the Congress. Cleavage between the executive and legislative branches first became noticeable in the summer of 1861. Initial disharmony was due in part to disagreement over appointments. Fire-eaters thought the

President gave too many offices to anti-secessionists and anti-secessionists in turn accused him of showing partiality to the fire-eaters. Delegations from one state complained that their constituents were being neglected in favor of those of another. Some of the generals had admirers in Congress who were quick to denounce any mistreatment, fancied or real, of their military heroes. Beauregard had an especially strong following in Congress: Wigfall, Pryor and Chesnut served as voluntary aides to him in 1861, and in February, 1862, his brother-in-law, Charles J. Villere, entered Congress. When the President and the "Grand Creole" had their first disagreement in the autumn of 1861 over who was to blame for not following up the victory at Manassas, Beauregard's partisans in Congress jumped to his defense and heaped denunciation on the President's head. Some of them even accused the President of having gone to the battlefield on the day of the fight with a view of stealing the glory from Beauregard and Johnston.

Beauregard's correspondence indicates that he kept in close touch with his friends in Congress, and that he did not hesitate to seek their aid in time of need. In following this course he was by no means unique among Confederate generals. Even the pious Jackson asked the assistance of his Congressman, A. R. Boteler, on several occasions and once obtained Boteler's interposition in a quarrel with Secretary Benjamin.

The Mallory diary indicates that wives had a part in the initial estrangement of President and Congress. On June 12, 1861, the Navy- Secretary noted: "At the [dining] table devoted to the Pres'd't and Cabinet and his company, Mr. [and] Mrs. Wigfall also sit; and Mrs. Wigfall evidently has determined to *snub* Mrs. Davis and her sister Miss Howel[l]. Her manner is a perfect rebuke and her air one of toleration and sufferance. But Mrs. D. and Miss H. are the last women to take such an exhibition quietly; and consequently there is a perpetual cross fire of sharpshooting in an amicable way. Cutting things are said blandly; and quiet smiles . . . cover rifle balls." On June 14 Mallory wrote: "More squabbles and covert sarcasm at table. Mrs. Wigfall evidently thinks that Mrs. Davis regrets her presence at table and she affects great indifference if not contempt from [for] all

Mrs. Davis says." The entry for June 23 reports a truce between the feminine contestants, but the feud smouldered on and probably contributed to the rupture which occurred between Davis and Senator Wigfall a few months later and which eventually developed into one of the bitterest antagonisms known to the Confederacy. Other women were drawn into the controversy, including Mrs. Joseph E. Johnston, who was an intimate of the Wigfalls, and the Quartermaster General's wife, the beautiful Mrs. Myers, who, as previously stated, did her husband irreparable injury by calling Mrs. Davis an "old squaw." Varina Davis's situation was made the more difficult by the seclusion forced on her by the President's frail health, the jealousy which her position naturally aroused, and the inclination of the Virginia blue-bloods, with whom Mrs. Joseph E. Johnston associated, to despise the Western upbringing of the Confederacy's first lady.

Relations between Davis and Congress worsened considerably in the latter part of 1861, and by the following spring they had deteriorated to the point of open hostility on the part of many of the legislators. Several influences contributed to this heightening of antipathy, the most important of which was growing dissatisfaction with the President's conduct of the war. The series of defeats experienced by the South in the winter and spring were charged to Davis's addiction to dispersion and defense, and his reliance on incompetent advisors. His advocacy of conscription, impressment and the suspension of the writ of habeas corpus also alienated a goodly number of Congressmen, including some who in the interest of the common good cast their votes in favor of these measures.

The success of Davis in securing enactment of these and other administrative measures has tended to obscure the scope and intensity of the Congressional reaction against Davis that took place in 1862. Mrs. Davis in her memoir refers to the new Congress that assembled in February, 1862, as being less friendly to her husband than the group it superseded. She goes on to state: "Now for the first time there appeared to be an organized party in opposition to the Administration." This was putting the situation all too mildly. A piecing together of evidence gleaned from letters, diaries and other contemporary sources indicates that behind the scenes a strong and bitter attack was launched against the President in Congress, and that some who participated in it were determined to force Davis from office. On March 16, 1862, Thomas R. R. Cobb wrote his wife that Congress was secretly debating the deposition of Davis and added: *"He would be deposed* if the Congress had any more confidence in Stephens than in him."

The antagonists of Davis in Congress, realizing that prospects of getting rid of him were dim, set about to clip his wings. With a view of ousting the despised Benjamin and preventing the President's personal control of military operations they tried to secure the appointment of Lee as Secretary of War. Davis refused to make this change on the ground that the war office should be headed by a civilian. Congress then passed an act requiring the chief executive to appoint a commanding general who should have authority to take personal command of any field army at any time. Davis vetoed this measure on the ground that it violated his constitutional rights as commander-in-chief. At the same time he ordered Lee to Richmond and charged him under the President's direction with the conduct of the South's military operations. The President thus scored a victory over his Congressional enemies, for he used Lee in an advisory capacity only and continued to exercise as much control over operations as before. Congress did succeed in its efforts to force Benjamin from the war office, but this accomplishment was deprived of its appeasing effects when Davis on March 17, 1862, appointed Benjamin Secretary of State.

The President further antagonized Congress by his removal of Beauregard from command of the Army of Tennessee in June, 1862. As previously noted, fifty-nine of the legislators entered a written protest against the removal and the manner in which it was done. But when the protest was presented to the President by members of the Louisiana delegation he rejected it with a brusqueness that added fuel to the flame of congressional antipathy. . . .

The year of 1865 brought an increase of discord. In February Congress and the Virginia Legislature forced the resignation of Secretary Seddon and compelled Davis to make Lee general-in-chief of the armies. When the Congressmen adjourned on March 18, 1865, with the Union forces pressing in on the capital for the kill, they and the President were probably angrier with each other than at any prior period of the war.

*   *   *

Relations between Davis and his generals also left much to be desired. The most notable cases of disharmony were those of the President with Joseph E. Johnston and Beauregard. The first known rupture between the President and Johnston occurred in September, 1861. On August 31, 1861, Davis sent to the Senate the names of five officers for confirmation as full generals. Prior Confederate legislation had provided that the relative rank of these and other officers should be determined by their former commissions in the United States army. Johnston held the permanent rank of colonel in the old army, but when he became Quartermaster General in 1860 he was automatically promoted to brigadier general, as the new position called for that grade. Hence when Johnston resigned from the Federal service he was a brigadier general, and he was the only officer among those entering the Confederate army from the old service who held a general's rank at the time of resignation. He expected to be at the head of the list sent to the Senate on August 31, 1861. But Davis, according to an explanation made after the war, considered permanent rank as the only measure for determining seniority, and on that basis he listed the five nominees for general in this order: Samuel Cooper, Albert Sidney Johnston, Robert E. Lee, Joseph E. Johnston and P. G. T. Beauregard, and thus they were confirmed.

Davis' letter justified his action on the ground that the Quartermaster Generalcy was a staff position, carrying with it no right to command troops, and Johnston, had he remained in the Federal service, would have reverted to a colonelcy at the end of his staff tour. The applicable Confederate legislation, however, did not specify that generals were to be ranked by their line ratings, but simply stated that they would be rated according to their *commission* in the old army. Davis himself was responsible for the interpretation that made Johnston fourth instead of first among the Confederate generals. And he was inconsistent in the application of his formula, else Cooper, who had little line experience and whose promotions above captain had come in connection with staff positions, would have been given a lower rank. The top men, Cooper and Albert Sidney Johnston, were two of Davis's closest friends among the old army group.

When Joseph E. Johnston saw the listing of generals he was furious. He immediately wrote an 1800-word protest to the President; after holding it for two days to allow himself to cool off, he sent it forward without change. It was now Davis's turn to be angry, and his temper must have boiled as he read the general's scathing charges that he had disregarded both law and justice in denying Johnston first place among the generals. Thirty-nine words sufficed for the President's response; it was one of the shortest letters that he ever wrote, but it was also one of the coldest. Dated September 14, 1861, it read: "Sir—I have just received and read your letter of the 12th instant. Its language is, as you say, unusual; its arguments and statements utterly one sided, and its insinuations as unfounded as they are unbecoming. I am, etc.—Jeff'n Davis."

Whatever their relations may have been before, there was no real harmony between Davis and Johnston after this angry flare-up of September, 1861. They were both proud and sensitive men, and they were honorable. But mutual trust, that essential ingredient of true concord, was gone from their relationship.

One has only to read their correspondence to sense the deep antagonism between them. In Johnston's view the authority of an army commander in time of war was virtually unlimited in the area of his jurisdiction. Hence he was annoyed by the President's seeming inclination to obtrude himself into the army's internal affairs. His extreme slowness in adopting Davis's insistent suggestion that regiments of the same state be brigaded together was doubtless due in part to a feeling that Davis was out of line in making such a proposal. And when Davis defended Benjamin in a quarrel that grew out of the Secretary's furloughing men and issuing orders to subordinate officers in the Army of Northern Virginia, Johnston was wrathful and understandably so.

Johnston's sensitiveness to prerogative and distrust of Davis, combined with a natural disposition to reticence, caused him to reveal very little of his activities and plans to the President, and this in turn was most annoying to Davis who often complained to the general and others that he was inadequately informed of Johnston's doings and intentions.

When Johnston recovered from his Seven Pines wound he desired more than anything else to return to his former command, or as he put it in a letter to Senator Wigfall "to be replaced where the Yankee missiles found me." Davis in assigning him instead to command of all the forces between the Appalachians and the Mississippi, including the armies of Bragg and Pemberton, insisted that he was giving him the highest military position in the Confederacy. But Johnston thought otherwise: Pemberton's and Bragg's forces were too far apart, he argued, to permit of effective command by one person; for an itinerant superior to take charge of them in succession would be impracticable and unfair both to the superior and to the army commander who was temporarily displaced. Johnston's letters to Wigfall reveal that he regarded the Western command not as an honor, but as a sort of glorified inspector generalship conferred by Davis to put him on the shelf. If Davis was sincere in his claim that the command was of prime importance, said Johnston, then he should give it to Lee, the Confederacy's first ranking field commander, and send him back to the Army of Northern Virginia. (Johnston's disappointment at not being returned to his old command on one occasion caused him to register a twinge of jealousy of Lee. On hearing of the Federal defeat at Fredericksburg he wrote Wigfall: "What luck some people have. Nobody will come to attack me in such a place.")

On January 3, 1863, after looking over his new command, Johnston restated to Davis his objections to the assignment and added: "With these views I earnestly beg some other position which may give me better opportunity to render such service as I may be capable of." But

Davis refused to transfer him and in so doing helped to set the stage for Vicksburg.

It is interesting to speculate on what might have happened if Lee had been sent west in December, 1863, and Johnston returned to the command of the Army of Northern Virginia. Lee probably would not have deemed the direction of two armies as impracticable as did Johnston; his greater tact would have brought more effective cooperation with Richmond; and his decisiveness and boldness might have caused greater difficulty for Grant and Rosecrans. Johnston, while a brilliant tactician, especially in defensive operations, would hardly have won such victories as those of Second Manassas and Chancellorsville; but at the same time he might have avoided such a costly defeat as Gettysburg. It seems reasonable to think that Johnston would have been more effective in the East than he was in the West, and that Lee's aggressive methods were more vitally needed in Mississippi than in Virginia. In view of all the factors involved, it appears unlikely that Pemberton's army would have been lost had Lee and Johnston changed places in December, 1862. But the shift probably would not have changed the outcome of the war.

These are only speculations. The fact remains that Johnston stayed on in the West. Misunderstanding and discord with Davis increased and Vicksburg was lost. After Vicksburg the war of words between the two became more intense, and Johnston grew firmer in the opinion that Davis held a grudge against him, would never give him real support and would use him as a scapegoat for the failure of others. He was sustained in these views by members of the anti-Davis clique in Congress, and especially by Wigfall, with whom he held frequent correspondence and whose hatred of the President raged with increasing fury. . . .

Congress and public opinion finally forced restoration of Johnston to command in February, 1865, but the change was made through the agency of Lee whom the President under pressure had appointed general-in-chief. Johnston and Davis were brought together briefly at Greensboro after Lee's surrender where in cold formality they exchanged opposing views as to future moves.

But peace with the Yankees did not bring a similar bless-
ing to the President and the general. They carried on
their private war for the rest of their lives. In 1885, four
years before he died, Davis stated in a letter to L. B.
Northrop: "Joe Johnston I see is to have an office under
the new Administration, so that rewards for treachery
have not ceased with radical rule." . . .

In the quarrels of Davis and his generals both sides
were at fault. But this fact did not diminish the bitterness
of these malignant controversies or lessen their injury to
the Southern cause.

*   *   *

Even more damaging to the Confederacy was the disharmony between Davis and the governors. At one time
or another the President came into conflict with most
of the state executives, and the issue was usually some
aspect of states' rights. These controversies, which were
especially serious in the cases of Brown and Vance,
have been ably treated by Professor Frank L. Owsley and
others, and it is not necessary to review them here. When
a government founded on the principle of states' rights
became engaged in a war that taxed to the utmost every
resource, considerable disagreement over national and
state prerogative was to be expected. But these disagree-
ments ought not to have degenerated into angry, irrecon-
cilable quarrels between state and national executives, and
the fact that they did reflects discreditably on all who
were involved. He who in the relative calm of the present
reads the correspondence of two honest, patriotic and
well-meaning men like Davis and Vance cannot but
be startled when he encounters a statement such as that
contained in the President's letter of March 31, 1864,
to the North Carolina governor. "There are other
passages of your letter," Davis wrote, "in which you
have so far infringed the proprieties of official intercourse as to preclude the possibility of reply. In order
that I may not again be subjected to the necessity of
making so unpleasant a remark, I must beg that a
correspondence so unprofitable in its character and
which was not initiated by me, may here end, and that
your future communications be restrained to such mat-

ters as may require official action." It is not surprising that subsequent correspondence between the two executives was infrequent and formal.

Disharmony between Davis and some of the newspaper editors was characterized by similar acrimony. Presidential relations with Rhett of the Charleston *Mercury* and Daniel and Pollard of the Richmond *Examiner* were especially bitter. The attacks of these editors had a strongly personal flavor and were sometimes flagrantly insulting in their tone. After the fall of Vicksburg, Daniel wrote a violent editorial attributing the catastrophe to the President's blind and stubborn attachment to Pemberton. "Had the people dreamed that Mr. Davis would carry all his chronic antipathies, his bitter prejudices, his puerile partialities, and his doting favoritisms into the presidential chair," he stated, "they would never have allowed him to fill it." . . .

The assumption that Confederates were excessively contentious naturally raises the question why? A number of reasons suggest themselves. One is the exaggerated individualism which the Southern way of life had nurtured from early colonial times. In New England geography and Puritanism fostered compact communities, interdependence and public discussion. In the South, climate and soil and an abundance of arable land promoted ruralism, and ruralism encouraged self-reliance and impeded the exchange of ideas. The introduction of slavery led to the establishment of the plantation system, and while planters were always a decided minority their prestige was such that they determined the pattern of behavior and set the tone of society. By law and by custom each planter became a petty sovereign. The chivalric code to which he subscribed made him hypersensitive to honor.

The domineering, individualistic quality which permeated Southern life was noted by many travellers who visited the land of Dixie in antebellum times. Alexis de Toqueville, for example, in his *Democracy in America*, observed that: "The citizen of the Southern states becomes a sort of domestic dictator from infancy; the first notion he acquires in life is that he was born to command, and the first habit he contracts is that of ruling without resistance. His education tends, then, to give him the character of a haughty and hasty man—irascible, violent, ardent in his desires, impatient of obstacles." . . .

Whatever its origins and foundations, there can be no doubt that individualism was always strong in the South; by the time the Confederacy was established it had reached such a point among the upper classes that almost every man seemed inclined to think himself more capable of directing public affairs than those charged with that responsibility. Certainly the concept of full cooperation, of following the leader, of functioning as a member of the team, was very, very weak. On February 5, 1861, while the Confederate government was in process of organization, James H. Hammond wrote his good friend William Gilmore Simms: *"Big-man-me-ism* reigns supreme and every one thinks every other a jealous fool or an aspiring knave." The characteristic which he dubbed so expressively was destined to increase. One who reads the writings of the period sometimes gets the impression that the aristocratic Southerner who staunchly supported the Davis government after the first year of war was a rarity. "Died of Big-man-me-ism" would not be an inappropriate epitaph for the Southern Confederacy.

A second possible reason for excessive contentiousness among Confederates was habit, developed during the long and bitter controversy with the North over slavery and states rights. Southerners participated in this controversy with greater feeling and in relatively greater numbers than Northerners because they were the minority and a dwindling one at that, because they regarded the threat to slavery as a direct menace to their way of life and because they had more leisure for brooding and recrimination than did Northerners. The slavery controversy was in a sense merely incidental to the life of Northerners who especially in the 1840's and 1850's were deeply absorbed in industrial development, westward expansion and the accumulation of wealth, while to Southerners this controversy was life itself. So, denunciation of the North became a major industry among Southerners in the decades before the war, and quarreling was deeply ingrained in their mode of life.

After secession removed the North as a principal source of contention, Southerners, from long addiction to controversy, turned on each other. To be sure there was a honeymoon of harmony, but before they had been under their own government a year, they were attacking Jefferson Davis and other Confederate leaders as vehemently as they had ever denounced the Yankees.

A third cause of dissension among Confederates was frustration. A "nation with nothing" found that the waging of a great war with a country rich in all essential resources was a formidable undertaking. Improvisation and skimping were fun at first, and early successes on the battlefield inspired an assurance that inconveniences would be short-lived. But when self-sacrifice and devotion failed to bring quick victory, the public mood changed. New measures, calling for increased inconvenience and self-denial, were resorted to by the government, with hopeful statements as to consequences. What resulted was not a turn of the tide but greater disaster and increased deprivation. As months passed into years, and the South grew weaker while the North appeared stronger and more determined, an ever increasing number of Southerners realized the hopelessness of their cause. The prospect of defeat was exceedingly embittering. In their disillusionment and disappointment the people became more and more irritable and testy. They sought scapegoats for their unhappy and unexpected plight. In their frustration they lashed out at each other, and angry, unreasoning controversy became rife throughout the Confederacy.

Another possible cause of inordinate quarrelsomeness among Confederates was a sense of guilt about slavery. The Old South was orthodox, Calvinist and evangelical. Its people were acutely aware of sin and believed strongly that divine displeasure and punishment were normal consequences of wrongdoing. . . .

Part X

THE ECONOMIC BREAKDOWN

26. Frank E. Vandiver: THE LOGISTICS OF SOUTHERN DEFEAT *

(Editor's note: Mr. Vandiver analyzes six factors which complicated the command picture: (1) the geographic pattern of the Confederate States, (2) manpower, (3) leadership, (4) economy, (5) Southern attitude toward the war, and (6) communications.)

What combined effect did all these factors have on the command? Essentially, they retarded the recognition of command's basic nature. The war, it was soon apparent, was not to be short. The longer it lasted, the more obvious became the weaknesses of the Confederacy. The more these were recognized, the more each branch of the war effort desperately sought to bolster its own position, with little consideration for other branches.

The new Federal "Anaconda" policy, exerting pressure all along the Confederate line, brought out a new concept of war for which the South found itself wholly unprepared. Such total war, in which everybody was a cog in a national war effort, was a surprise. Civilian morale was now as important as soldier morale; civilian resistance as important as military resistance. The need for all types of supplies could only be met by full-scale civilian production. The dream of a Walter Scott South did not die at Appomattox—it died in the furnaces and clothing mills of a maximum war effort. It died when Southern women copied the "wage slaves" of Lowell and made bullets, arms, and uniforms, as well as bandages.

The transition was too much. It came too fast. Jefferson Davis began to see the need of a centralized govern-

* Frank E. Vandiver, *Rebel Brass* (Baton Rouge: Louisiana State University Press, 1956), pp. 18-23. Reprinted by permission.

ment to fight the war, but even he was unaware of how far this might have to go. Struggling to fight a national war amid state rights ideas was an impossible task. Total war could not be waged piecemeal.

But it was with a piecemeal approach that the Confederacy departmentalized its effort, not only governmentally, but militarily. Generals of various field forces had to fend for themselves in isolated areas. Richmond, to which all looked for guidance, was the nerve center of the Confederacy, but a nerve center lacking the power of co-ordination. Distances were too great and communications too slow. Various schemes were tried to overcome this estrangement, but none was fully successful.

Gradually, whole areas drifted out of the Richmond orbit. The Trans-Mississippi Department, after the fall of Vicksburg, was to all practical purposes lost. Richmond authorities could never be certain that communications reached this area, and it was so remote from the capital that the government dared not direct operations about which it could know so little.

What happened to the Trans-Mississippi Department happened elsewhere. Bits and dribbles of the manpower reserve were siphoned off here and there to hold first one spot and then another. Eventually, the middle Confederacy—east Louisiana, Mississippi, and Alabama— was under only nominal control from Richmond. The combination of distance and geography resulted in splintering the South.

It seems doubtful that anyone in the Confederate hierarchy understood the real nature of the command problem. Command was a function which could be delegated, but not abdicated, by the government. Everything about a war effort is basically a command problem, and nothing going on in a country is beyond the scope of strategic high command planning. This was certainly true in the Confederacy. If the real nature of the problem had been understood early in the war it would have been clear that there were no isolated actions. No general could be allowed to fend for himself without doing violence to the scheme of the war. War, by the 1860's, had taken on a new aspect. It was now a phenomenon of extensive and rapid movement, which gave rise to a new dimension in the old science of logistics. Mass movements of mass armies and supplies involved the whole economy and all of society. Consequently, everything was a command responsibility.

Co-ordination is a basic ingredient of high command. The frequent references in contemporary literature to Confederate "armies" are more accurate than they first appear to be. There was no real "Army" during the whole war. The Secretary of War and the Adjutant General did very little to co-ordinate operations. In addition, there was, as usual, practically no co-operation between the army and navy. Both the Secretary of War and the Secretary of the Navy went their own separate ways.

Confederate failure to recognize, in time to make any difference, that war had become a national experience reflects the lack of strategic planning, not a want of foresight. Over-all direction of the Southern war effort was never provided. A general staff might have been the answer, but it was never tried. There is some evidence, however, that as the war progressed the Confederate government began to see the need for some type of comprehensive command. Several experiments were tried in an effort to obtain limited, but still largely local, co-ordination of military operations. Efficient and quick integration of the military and nonmilitary aspects of war was too much to expect of a nation dedicated to decentralization.

27. John C. Ropes: STEAM AND ELECTRICITY *

In the beginning of this paper we spoke of the magnitude of the task which the North proposed to itself. It was not without apparent reason that the world doubted and smiled in derision at the presumption of the Northern Government in thinking that it could succeed in such a gigantic undertaking. Was it possible that a nation with such an insignificant navy could establish an effec-

* John C. Ropes, "The War as We See It Now," in Theodore F. Dwight, ed., *Critical Sketches of Some of the Federal and Confederate Commanders* (Boston: Houghton Mifflin & Co., 1895), pp. 268-272.

tive blockade over three thousand miles of sea-coast? Did the Northern generals suppose that armies, large enough to overcome the fierce and universal resistance which was to be expected, could live on the country they were invading? And if not, did not the great distances to be traversed render the problem of transportation and subsistence well-nigh an insurmountable one? Some successes, no doubt, the great superiority of the North in men and material might enable it to win; very possibly the boundary might be pushed back a certain distance. But for the Northern forces to overrun the South, or to follow up the Southern armies into the interior of the country, and there to maintain themselves in the midst of an unfriendly population and on a soil in great part destitute of the means of subsistence, as a great portion of the Southern Confederacy unquestionably was, seemed to many disinterested and clear headed men of those days well-nigh impracticable. It is true that neither Lord Palmerston nor the Emperor Napoleon the Third inclined to the side of the North; nevertheless we believe that it was not by any means wholly due to their unwillingness to see us succeed that they predicted our failure. We believe that they judged the probabilities of the case by the light of experience; and, judging by the light of experience, it was not likely that the North would succeed if the South should resolutely persist in endeavoring to maintain her independence by force of arms. Lord Palmerston and the Emperor of the French were probably as well qualified to have an opinion on this subject as any two men in Europe; the one had been Secretary at War from 1809 to 1815, in the time of the first Napoleon; the other, although not a soldier himself, had been a diligent and intelligent student of the campaigns of his great uncle. Both these experts predicted the failure of the North. And it may safely be admitted that if the conditions of warfare had been the same in 1861 as they were in 1815, or, in our judgment, as late as 1850, their prediction would in all probability have been fulfilled.

But the conditions were not the same. Steam and electricity had in the intervening time asserted their power, and had rendered possible for a McClellan or a Grant what had been impossible for a Napoleon. It was found that the capacity of the territory, through which it was proposed to move an army, for the task of supporting that army might generally be disregarded. It was found perfectly feasible to maintain a large force for any length of time in regions where no subsistence of any sort or kind was furnished by the soil. It was found that water-transportation of men and supplies was as certain and uniform, as much to be relied upon, as transportation by land; that the winds and waves of the ocean and the strength and direction of the flow of rivers could equally be ignored when it was proposed to transport troops, or subsistence, or ammunition, to a given spot. It was found that a blockade maintained by steam vessels, though not absolutely perfect, was a far more certain and constant check on foreign intercourse than could be effected by any employment of sailing vessels. By the telegraph all available resources could be utilized without the loss of a moment, and all information instantaneously communicated to or from headquarters to or from any part of the theatre of war. In other words, machinery had in the progress of time become one of the great factors in military operations, and its introduction worked as marked a revolution in the practice of commanders on land and sea, as its adoption for purposes of manufacture or of intercommunication had worked in the world of business and ordinary life. And, what was of the greatest importance to the North, the advantages of this great change in matters of warfare were absolutely at the call of the stronger and more wealthy of the two combatants.

There had been but little in the way of example to follow. Steam-vessels had, it is true, supplied in great part the allied armies in the Crimea. There had also been a short railroad constructed for the accommodation of the English from Balaklava to the front, but it had taken a great while to build, and it was not very serviceable after it was built. The French and Austrians had also used their railroads in the short Italian war of 1859. But there was really not much to serve as a precedent.

The task of developing the possibilities of the use of steam and electricity in warfare was, therefore, first tried on a large scale in the war of secession. Naturally and inevitably it fell to the North to deal with the subject with the greater thoroughness and ingenuity of application. For the North could overcome the great natural difficulties presented by the geographical conditions under which the war was to be carried into the Confederacy only by utilizing to the full the vast resources it possessed through the powerful agency of steam, and the incalculable assistance afforded by the electric telegraph. And it will probably be conceded without demur, that no people ever lived more capable of making ingenious and useful applications of steam and electricity to war or to anything else, than the people of the Northern States.

The first thing to do was to enlarge the navy so as to compass a blockade of the Southern coast, and the next thing was to build a navy for use on the great rivers which run through the heart of the Confederacy. That both tasks were successfully accomplished in a very brief period reflects the greatest credit on the officers of the navy. We have not time here, nor is this the place, to give the details; but in a couple of months or thereabouts the blockade had become reasonably effective on the Atlantic seaboard and in the Gulf of Mexico; and, partly by purchasing river steamers and refitting them, and partly by building new and armor-plated vessels, the Federal Government, early in 1862, had procured a fleet on the Mississippi and its tributaries, which laid those great avenues into the interior of the South open to the Northern invaders. The first fruit of the employment of this naval force in conjunction with the army was the capture of Fort Donelson in February, 1862, with its entire garrison, entailing the evacuation, by the Confederate General A. S. Johnston, of the greater part of the States of Kentucky and Tennessee.

The task of providing subsistence and forage for the armies of both the North and South during the long months of winter and spring, when the roads were well-nigh impassable and the surrounding country afforded next to nothing which could be of service, was immensely simplified by railroads. It might be thought at first sight that the advantage of this arrangement lay with the army which was on the defensive, as their opponents would naturally be obliged to cut loose from their railroad communications in any forward movement. But it should be considered that the all-important thing for the North, whose resources so immeasurably exceeded those of the South, was to maintain as large an army as it could get together at a point from which, as soon as the season opened, operations could be successfully commenced; and that railroads and steamboats made it always possible for the North to accomplish this. Thus, during the winter of 1864 and 1865, somewhere near 130,000 men were comfortably quartered and supplied in the Federal lines from Bermuda Hundred to Petersburg, in a country where absolutely nothing was furnished from the soil or by the inhabitants; and when the time came, Grant was able to open the campaign with an overwhelming superiority of force. If the railroads now in operation in Russia had existed in Napoleon's day, it may well be believed that he would have supplied his immense army with subsistence and forage during the winter of 1812 and 1813, and would have made a success of his invasion. And, it may equally well be believed, that, had it not been for the railroads in France, the Prussians could never have maintained during the winter of 1870 and 1871 the enormous army which surrounded and finally reduced Paris. . . .

28. Charles W. Ramsdell: GENERAL ECONOMIC WEAKNESSES OF THE CONFEDERACY *

The industrial weakness of the South was one of the decisive factors in its defeat, not merely because of the appalling scarcity of so many essential articles—even of such common things as axes, spades, hammers, nails, pins, needles, plows, hoes, horseshoes, steam engines, wool and cotton clothing, shoes, harness, wagons, and scores of other commonplace necessities—but also because the colonial economy which had been so characteristic of southern business before the war had left the country without sufficient fluid capital or coin to sustain the currency. Foreign purchases, as well as paper treasury

* Charles W. Ramsdell, *Behind the Lines in the Southern Confederacy* (Baton Rouge: Louisiana State University Press, 1944), pp. 103-104, 113-120. Reprinted by permission.

notes, had drained out the specie. The absence of a "mixed industry" is merely a part of the whole hopeless situation. The danger came to be thoroughly understood soon after the war began, and efforts were made to fill the gap when it was too late. "It is the northern mechanic," said one southerner, "who is defeating us." . . .

As we look backward over what had happened it becomes very clear that the southern people had not been able to solve the internal problems which the war had raised. *Could* they have solved them if they had been able to anticipate them and if they had adopted other measures? That is a hard question, but my present conviction is that only a series of miracles would have made it possible. If they had been opposed to a power of no more than equal strength, they might have won; but they were constantly forced to exert their utmost strength, and every mistake was costly. The strain on their resources was terrific and the government had no choice but to sacrifice one interest to another, the one which seemed of less immediate concern to that which seemed greater. To most of the higher army officers and to Davis himself, keeping the army at full strength in order to hold the enemy at bay naturally seemed the most important thing, but this is not to say that they were indifferent to or neglected other considerations. For instance, it seems clear enough that both Congress and the President made a sincere effort to work out a system of selective service for the army that would do the least damage possible to the economic and social structure upon which the armies must rest; but they were without precedent or experience or any accurate means of analyzing the needs of the civilian population. And they had failed to take into account the class jealousies aroused by certain exemptions such as the twenty-Negro clause provided in the conscription acts. When they tried later to remedy these errors, if they were errors, the damage was already done and could not be corrected. The Confederate government moved steadily, if rather slowly in some matters, toward more and more control over the ordinary activities of the people, but it was the desperate situation that forced it in this direction. Of course this development aroused opposition but there was criticism on the other hand because the government did not move rapidly enough.

The state governments also wrestled with these internal difficulties and greatly extended their control over matters formerly regarded as outside the functions of government. These things they did not only in the interest of their own people but also in behalf of the common cause and to assist the efforts of the Confederate government. Much has been said about the controversies over state rights within the Confederacy—and of course there were such controversies—but it needs to be pointed out that the state governments, including the individual governors, exerted themselves far more in loyally assisting the general government than in thwarting it. And in these policies the state governments were sustained by the mass of the people.

But let us look back at these internal problems upon whose solution depended the maintenance of the southern struggle for political independence. One, perhaps the most important, was that of finances. Here there was complete failure and the wonder is that the government was able to hold up for so long after its credit and currency had utterly collapsed. The war had to be financed on credit; but there was no basis for such an amount of credit except the staple crops, and they could not be utilized to any great extent because of the blockade and the lack of a navy strong enough to break that blockade. Granted that there were initial mistakes on the part of the states as well as of the Confederate government in resorting to treasury notes and bonds, these measures were exactly those which any people with small monetary resources and hopeful of early peace were likely to adopt. And what else could they have done? We have seen how many of the later difficulties followed as a consequence of disordered finances.

All efforts to check price inflation proved futile. Some of them, such as embargoes and seizures of speculators' goods, were bound to fail. There could have been no remedy for inflated prices but a sound currency, ample production, and an adequate system of transportation. The limitation of cotton and tobacco planting, though not perfectly administered, seems to have had good effects. Enough food was produced, but it could not be distributed where it was needed. The relief measures adopted by the states unquestionably did much good, but they never worked with entire satisfaction because of the loss of purchasing power in the currency, the disturbances incident to wartime, the difficulties in getting food, salt, and clothing to those in need, and the forced resort to the clumsy method of bartering for supplies. The consequence was plenty in some communities and near starvation in others. Nevertheless, all things considered, it is hard to see how the authorities could have done more.

But impressments, one result of currency troubles, were extremely unpopular and it is a question whether they did as much good as harm. They did not check the ruinous rise of prices and they did in far too many cases deprive plantations and farms, factories and shops, of the means of greater production and they helped to break down the railroad service. Worse still, they outraged the feelings of hitherto loyal people, leaving with them a bitter sense of wanton injustice. Of course, this was not the intention of the authors of the impressment policy, but the execution of the law was left in the hands of men who, in the nature of their work, could not be closely supervised, who were concerned only in getting supplies in the easiest way, who had no local responsibility, and who, more and more, became demoralized by opportunities for speculation. No other one thing, not even conscription, caused so much discontent and produced so much resentment toward the Confederacy.

The transportation problem, also a vital matter to both the people and the armies, was never properly diagnosed. The inherent difficulties were enormous, but had there been foresight and intelligent planning at the beginning, the railroads could have stood up better under the strain. After Quartermaster General Alexander R. Lawton had virtually taken over control of the roads at the end of 1863, he and some of his subordinates did what was possible to rehabilitate the lines, but it was then too late. The railroad officials themselves, representing a multitude of small lines, were never able to co-ordinate their policies and services, and when the army and state officials tried to remedy the faults of train service by force, their interference too often resulted merely in disrupting it. There were no men trained in railway economics or in operation on a large scale. It was all a sort of rule-of-thumb business. Probably railway development had not then reached the stage for centralized control, but the lack of any such control, except such as the quartermaster general exercised, prevented a solution of the problem. As to local transportation by wagons and teams, I have already explained that the inability to make wagons as fast as they broke down, the wear and tear on the horse and mule supply in army service, and the impressment of a large portion of those that were needed in agriculture and in hauling crops left this essential service paralyzed.

Trade with the outer world went through the same transition from unregulated private enterprise, which fostered speculation, to state trade activities, and finally to Confederate control during the last year. The Confederate law of February 6, 1864, by which the President was empowered to establish regulations for all export and import trade, was less an attempt to extend the power of the government than it was to put an end to waste of resources on useless importations and to provide supplies for the army that could not otherwise be had. It extended the President's power and not only aroused the opposition of thoroughly loyal governors by interfering with their own activities in behalf of their people, but also gave opportunity to the critics of Davis to charge him with dictatorial ambitions. Strangely enough, it had been urged early in the war that the government do this very thing, but it was not done until the last year. The plan did not work satisfactorily because the regulations imposed did not fit the situation of all regions. It did not work well in Texas, for instance, where the commanding general of the Trans-Mississippi Department had established a Cotton Bureau on different principles, which, because of the peculiar situation there, were really preferable to the President's regulations. But because the law prescribed uniformity, Davis forced the dissolution of General Kirby-Smith's Cotton Bureau. And on the Atlantic and Gulf coasts the blockade was tightening down so that the great days of blockade-running were past. Confederate control came too late to accomplish much for the government.

As to the illegal trade with the enemy, we have already seen how futile were the efforts to stop it; but it is interesting to see to what lengths the efforts went—arrest and imprisonment of the traders, at times; the confiscation of the cotton, at times. But the stakes were so high, and the methods of control were so inefficient, that the traffic was checked but little, except where the military was strong enough to seize all the cotton itself and do its own trading on army account.

Summing it all up, it can be said that the southern people and their governments failed, with a few exceptions, to conserve, develop, and efficiently administer their resources; but it must be said that these were gigantic tasks, intricate, complex, and baffling. That they did not succeed better is not surprising when we remember the simplicity of southern economic and political organization before secession. There was not time, while a powerful and determined enemy was crashing at the gate, to reorganize their whole system and, without previous experience, develop a far-reaching and studied policy, create a complex administration, and train administrators. Problems had to be met as they arose; and unexpected problems arose with bewildering rapidity, demanding instant solution. All in all, it is not surprising that they could not be solved, or that, in the end, the collapse was complete. . . .

Part XI

THE BREAKDOWN OF TRANSPORTATION

29. Charles H. Wesley: THE FAILURE OF THE RAILROAD *

During the opening periods of the war, the railroad companies, expecting an early termination of the war, placed their reliance upon the stocks which they had on hand; and consequently they made little effort to replenish them. Soon all roads were suffering for want of cars and engines. The few shops which could repair cars and engines had been taken over by the government to be used for war purposes. The government's opinion was that the railroads should take care of their own repairs; and, being imbued with laissez-faire doctrines, it took no part in the repairs of the roads until necessity demanded it. By degrees the necessity of supervision arose; and in 1861, W. S. Ashe, formerly president of the Wilmington and Weldon Railroad, was appointed with the rank of major to direct the transportation of troops. In 1862, Colonel Wadly was assigned to the supervision and control of troops on all railroads. His powers were more extensive than those of Ashe, but his nomination was not agreed to by the Senate. In 1863, General Lawton was made Quartermaster-General and Colonel Sims was appointed in charge of railroads. This type of supervision while conferring with the individual roads was as far as the government went until February, 1865, when an act was passed authorizing the Secretary of War, to place any railroad, canal, or telegraph line under such officers as he should direct and to render any necessary aid or repair equipment. This was passed too late in the war to be of any consequence.

Gradually the tracks and the road equipment wore

* Charles H. Wesley, *The Collapse of the Confederacy* (Washington, 1937), pp. 38-41. Reprinted by permission.

out, and smaller lines were torn up in order to replenish the larger ones. Speed was sacrificed in order to save the roads. Passenger trains were limited to one or two a day in the latter part of 1864. Some of the railroads seemed, however, to be prospering financially. The Richmond and Petersburg Railroad Company paid a dividend of 15 per cent, in December, 1864. The North Carolina Railroad Company declared a semi-annual dividend of 25 per cent, in February, 1865. The Richmond and Danmain line extending between Savannah and Macon and the Richmond and Petersburg Railroad later declared a dividend of 10 per cent.

The physical situation of the roads became serious in 1864. The various presidents had urged Congress to allot the shops and the mechanics to be employed in railroad repair work, but these requests were not granted. The companies themselves were also too absorbed with particularism to unite their efforts and have their work done by such workmen as they could obtain. In the same year, General Lawton wrote that the fact could not be disguised that the railroads were in a critical condition and that the needs of transportation must continue to cause greater anxiety as the war progressed. The report of the Quartermaster-General in 1864 revealed the fact that a train could be kept in continuous daily service for only one hundred miles and that at the end of five hundred miles a breakdown could be expected in the cars.

In addition to the lack of mechanics and the condition of the roads, there was also the lack of materials. Colonel Sims, writing in February, 1865, stated that new cars were being built under difficulty but that new engines could not be manufactured in the Confederacy. He concluded that "not a single bar of railroad iron had been rolled in the Confederacy since the war." Nevertheless there was plenty of iron in Northern Alabama, Tennessee, North Carolina and South Carolina, which could have been extracted. Many locomotives needed tires, but somehow tires could not be secured, due, as Colonel Sims said, to the fact that the work of the shops was absorbed by the government for war purposes. He said that every important article of consumption by the railroads could be produced in the Confederate states and what the roads asked was iron ore, permission for foundries, rolling-mills and a liberal system of detailing machinists from the army.

Beginning in 1863, there was competition between the government plants and private factories for labor. Many machinists had left the South while others who remained were conscripted for the army. Colonel Sims reported that the hardships of war and the fear of conscription had induced many to leave, and in so doing, "they felt but little or no interest in our country or cause." Since the impressment of soldiers necessitated the closing of several factories, it was the opinion of some that Negro labor could be substituted for those who were impressed. The Tredegar Iron Works had employed several hundred Negroes in 1863-4, but it was feared that dissension would arise among them.

These conditions among the railroads were made worse by the invasion of southern territory by Union armies. General Sherman's army destroyed about 136 miles of mail line extending between Savannah and Macon and the branch lines to Augusta and Eatonsville. The crossties were burned and the rails were placed on top of the burning pile so that they could be twisted by the heat and made useless for practical purposes. In North Carolina and in South Carolina, it was said, the roads had become worthless by 1864. In Florida, Mississippi, Louisiana, and Tennessee, there were lines which escaped complete destruction, but they had so deteriorated that they could not be used for practical purposes. According to a report by Colonel S. R. Hamil, which was made on September 30, 1867, twenty-one railroads in the Southern states suffered losses during the war amounting to $28,187,404. . . .

30. Clement Eaton: THE TRANSPORTATION BREAKDOWN *

One of the most serious causes of the economic collapse of the Confederacy was the breakdown of the rail-

* Reprinted with permission of The Macmillan Company from *A History of the Southern Confederacy,* pp. 253-256, 258-259, by Clement Eaton. Copyright 1954 by Clement Eaton.

roads. The Southern railroads in 1860 were totally un-
suited to meet the strain of war. The system consisted
of a congeries of small railroads operated by at least
113 weak companies, the longest line under the control
of one company being the Mobile and Ohio with 469
miles of track. Practically all were owned by Southerners,
the notable exceptions being the Northern-owned Bruns-
wick and Florida in southern Georgia, which Governor
Brown seized in 1861 and operated under state authority,
and the Florida Railroad. These fragmentary railroads
had eleven different gauges, ranging from three feet to
five feet, six inches, making it impossible for the cars
and locomotives of some lines to traverse the tracks of
others. Fortunately, there was a continuous five-foot
gauge on lines running from New Orleans, Mobile, and
Memphis to Chattanooga and from there to Petersburg.
All the railroads were single-track, and most of them
had very inadequate sidings to permit the passage of
trains going in the opposite direction. The sharp curves,
the frail bridges and trestles, the waiting on sidings, the
necessity of frequent stops for cordwood fuel, slowed
the trains to about twelve miles an hour. The rails—some
of them of the T wrought-iron type, but others merely
thin iron straps on wooden stringers—were in general
flimsy, and wore out under the volume of war freight.
Furthermore, the railroad companies were inadequately
supplied with engines and cars, the largest numbers of
locomotives being owned by the South Carolina Railroad,
with 62, and the Central of Georgia, with 59. The South
Carolina Railroad had 849 cars as contrasted with the
4,000 owned by a single Northern company, the Delaware and Lackawanna.

At the beginning of the conflict representatives of
thirty-three railroads met in convention at Montgomery,
April 26, 1861, to adopt a uniform policy toward the
new government. They resolved to transport troops for
two cents per mile (the regular rate was three and one-
half cents), and to carry government freight for half the
amount charged to private business. Moreover, they
agreed for their companies to accept Confederate bonds
at par value in payment for services. These arrangements
were later accepted by a convention of Virginia railroads.
But the mood of patriotic abnegation soon passed, and

the Chattanooga railroad convention of October 4, 1861, raised rates for government transportation above the charges for private individuals. Although some Confederate railroads made huge paper profits and paid prodigious dividends, the profits were illusory for rolling stock and track were steadily deteriorating without ability of replacement.

As the war progressed, the Confederate and state governments practically monopolized the use of the railroads. In the concluding year the Virginia Central Railroad, for example, transported seven-eighths of its freight and two-thirds of its passengers for "government account." Before 1861 the Virginia Central had declared a semi-annual dividend of 2 per cent on its capital (nearly four million dollars); but in 1864 its president declared, "The stock holders of the railroad companies generally, are probably the only persons in the Confederacy whose capital has not been productive since the war began." In evaluating war profits it is well to remember that the state governments were frequently large stockholders in Southern railroads; for example, the Virginia government owned a majority of the shares of stock of the Virginia Central and appointed three of its five directors.

The Confederacy encountered numerous difficulties in utilizing the railroads. In the first place, many Northern mechanics had returned home, and others had been turned off by the railroads during the depression that followed secession and the cotton embargo. Some of the latter had joined the army, thus depriving the railroads of valuable mechanical skill sorely needed for operation in war time. The War Department, moreover, pursued a stupid policy in regard to releasing skilled mechanics from the army for railroad repairs. The companies had great trouble in securing slaves for rough labor on their roadbeds. The Confederate authorities did not realize the imperative necessity of upkeep and repair of railroads and engines. They did not import railroad iron through the blockade, and Lieutenant Colonel Frederick W. Sims, the officer in the Quartermaster Corps directly in charge of railroads, lamented February 10, 1865, that "not a single bar of railroad iron" had been rolled since 1861. Rails were torn from branch lines to repair the more essential lines. Lack of repairs of track and rolling equipment brought frequent wrecks and the loss of many days in forwarding military supplies.

Many bottlenecks developed in the flow of supplies and soldiers to the battle front. At Richmond, Augusta, Savannah, Lynchburg, Charlotte, Wilmington, and Petersburg the railroads did not connect. Thus through freight had to be hauled by wagon and dray from one side of each city to the other. Because this condition was very profitable for hotels, transfer companies, and merchants, the cities were reluctant to have the lines joined. Furthermore, railroad companies did not relish entrusting their cars to other companies, so that freight had to be transferred from the cars of one company to those of another. The result was that troops and supplies were delayed for days, and quartermaster and commissary supplies congested at the bottlenecks. The Virginia state convention authorized a connection through Petersburg, June 26, 1861; but the people of that city opposed a permanent connection, and the railroads did not wish to invest money in a flimsy temporary connection. Finally in August it was completed with Confederate funds—but with the proviso that private freight should not be transported over this link and that the tracks must be removed at the conclusion of the war. The route from Chattanooga over the mountains to Richmond was interrupted at Lynchburg by a difference of gauge. The Quartermaster General endeavored to obtain cars and engines from other roads to place on the line from Chattanooga to Lynchburg, the breadline of the Confederacy, but the jealousy of the individualistic railroads prevented this move.

The Confederate leaders did not recognize the supreme need for the government to take vigorous control over the railroads; and the laissez-faire ideas of the people and their devotion to constitutionalism militated against government seizure. Consequently, the numerous small railroads continued to operate under private management. In the first two years of the war Quartermaster General Abraham C. Myers, who had charge of transportation of the Confederate armies, was strongly opposed to government operation of the railroads. Bitterly criticized for his conduct of his department, he was replaced in August, 1863, by Brigadier General A. R. Lawton. Although these two officers had general supervision over the railroads, their control was exerted chiefly by negotiating contracts. The Confederate government did not attempt to fix passenger fares or freight rates for private individuals or businesses; but it did enforce priority of government over private freight. . . .

On February 28, 1865, when the war was practically lost, the Confederate Congress authorized the Secretary of War to assume control of any railroad needed for military purposes, transfer rolling stock or equipment from one railroad to another, tear up rails on branch lines and use them on main lines, and build new railroads. Employees and officers of the railroad companies were classified as part of the armed forces of the Confederacy. This law was a belated adoption of the practice of the United States government, which had given military superintendents of railroads, such as Herman Haupt and Daniel McCallum, extraordinary war powers to seize and operate all railroads and utilize all equipment needed for military transportation.

The transportation problem in the Confederacy was much larger than the inadequacy of the railroads. Before the outbreak of war a vast amount of freight had been carried in coastal vessels and river boats; but the blockade, the lack of repair facilities for ships, and the control of important rivers by the Federal Army seriously interrupted this traffic. There was great dependence also on horses, mules, oxen, and wagons, and the impressment officers interfered by taking draft animals. Oxen which the farmers used for draft were slaughtered for food. The scarcity of horseshoes prevented efficient use of work horses and even of cavalry and artillery mounts. Wagons broke down, and parts for repair could not be secured. Impressment officers seized the substantial wagons of the farmers, leaving only rickety and infirm vehicles.

In the Wigfall Papers are copies of letters from the various bureau chiefs, dated March 10-11, 1865, to Secretary of War Breckinridge describing the prospects for supplying the Army. The Ordnance chief reported that he could supply a moderate amount of ordnance as long as the Wytheville lead mines were held. Most of the Confederate armories had been broken up so that it was necessary to import arms through Florida. The chief of the Nitre and Mining Bureau reported that the Confederacy had enough nitre, lead, and sulphur for five months, but that there was a great deficiency in iron owing to lack of transportation. The Quartermaster General declared that Sherman's destruction of the rail line in South Carolina prevented transport of the abundant supplies of grain in Georgia and Alabama for the army animals, but that there was enough forage in North Carolina and Virginia to supply the army for three months to come. The manufacture of wagons and ambulances kept up with the demand, but there was a dearth of animals. He observed that "the people are clamorous for money for supplies which has been repeatedly promised and not paid." Particularly significant was his remark that "a larger supply of clothing has been issued to the armies in the last three months than in any similar period of the war." The Army was better supplied with shoes than with any other article, and he was confident that there would be no serious lack of clothing. The two essentials for continuing to supply the Army, he stated, were money and protection of the railroads from raids.

The Commissary General expressed the opinion that suitable funds and protection of the rails would make it practical to keep the Army depots full; but a lack of "funds that will be received without compulsion" would paralyze all efforts. Transportation difficulties, he pointed out, made it impossible to place more than four days' rations in reserve for the Army of Northern Virginia. J. H. Claiborne, commissary for Virginia, observed that large food supplies could be obtained from hoarders, but only in exchange for gold. S. B. French, commissary at Wilmington, reported that with acceptable money and transportation the subsistence of the troops would be easy. . . .

31. Robert C. Black: A BRIEF SUMMARY OF THE RAILROAD SITUATION *

The Confederate States did not win the Civil War. Were the carriers of the South in any degree responsible for that failure? To this question the author can only answer—yes. Railroad transportation in the Confederacy suffered from a number of defects, all of which played a recognizable part in the southern defeat:

1. There were not enough railroads in the South, in terms of line miles, and they were not always in the right places, strategically.

2. There existed far too many gaps in what should have been continuous lines. Included here should be differences of gauge, though this was not an exclusively Confederate deficiency.

3. The southern ability to manufacture railroad supplies was much too low. In the face of a general lightness of construction, a distinct *initial* shortage of rolling stock, and an increasingly effective Federal blockade, this was an extremely serious, if not fatal, matter.

The shortcomings named above might have proved decisive in themselves, always assuming that the Federal power never lifted its pressure. So often does the advantage of interior lines entail a beleaguered fortress, suffering from shortages of everything except mobility! Germany has twice discovered this, to her sorrow. *But the Confederates by no means made the best use of what they had.* It is men who are most at fault when a war is lost—not locomotives, or cars, or even economic geography. And in so far as railroad logistics were concerned, the Confederates committed two major sins:

1. Railroad owners, managers, and even employees were unwilling to make serious sacrifice of their personal interests.

2. The Confederate Government was loath to enforce the kind of transportation policy the war effort demanded.

Calhoun's glorification of the individual state and his doctrine of the concurrent majority may have provided a satisfactory political philosophy for outnumbered southerners in the old Union, but they were hardly an effective

* Robert C. Black, *Railroads of the Confederacy* (Chapel Hill: University of North Carolina Press, 1952), pp. 294-295. Reprinted by permission.

engine of unity in the face of military attack. Such theories had, over the decades, so permeated the thinking of southerners that they stood in terror of their own creation at Richmond. Even the Confederate Government was too frequently afraid of itself. And in no field was it more pusillanimous than in its handling of the railroad problem. This inability to face unpleasant measures affected in some degree every person involved—Ashe, Wadley, Sims, Seddon, the Congress, even Jefferson Davis himself, "Southern nationalist" though he was. Indeed, the Confederate President was not to acquiesce in the enforcement of really rigid transportation regulations until Appomattox was hardly a month off.

Without either wholehearted public cooperation, or government coercion, it is practically impossible to wage a modern war. It is well to possess both of these things. The Confederacy had too little of either. The North could claim at least one of them in good measure—a powerful government that understood its own potentialities and was comparatively unafraid to use them.

It is here, if anywhere, that the story of the railroads of the Confederacy assumes a distinctive meaning. And though it be but a minor chapter in a huge tragedy, it still may be worth the telling as an object lesson for Americans. For it perhaps has not been sufficiently emphasized how extraordinarily *American* the Confederates were. Even their locomotives were of the western continent. Their clanging bells proclaimed their nativity.

Part XII

FINANCES

32. Walter Geer: THE FAILURE OF FINANCES *

Opinions have always differed, and probably always will, as to the reasons for the failure of the Southern States to achieve their independence. Northern writers generally assume that it was due to the larger population and greater resources of the Union; Southern authorities ascribe it to a want of perseverance, unanimity, and even of loyalty, on the part of the South.

The main cause, however, seems to have been the bad financial policy adopted by the Confederate Government. Mr. Davis and his Cabinet must have realized that a full treasury was necessary to defray the expenses of a great war; but they deliberately rejected the best means of raising money: the sale of the large and valuable cotton crop.

Statistics show that the cotton crop of 1860 amounted to nearly four million bales, and it is estimated that the South had on hand at the outbreak of the war about five million bales. During the war, "the price of cotton reached almost fabulous figures" in England. The mill-owners were finally forced to shut down entirely, and two million people were reduced to great distress. This cotton, if stored abroad at that time, could have been sold for at least $500,000,000, and probably for much more. The blockade of the Southern ports was proclaimed in May, 1861, but it was not at all effective until the following spring. There was thus a period of nearly twelve months during which shipments could easily have been made. "The sum raised in that way," writes General Johnston, "would have enabled the War Department to procure at once arms enough for half a million of men,

* Walter Geer, *Campaigns of the Civil War* (New York: Brentano's, 1926), pp. 446-447. Reprinted by permission.

and after that expenditure the Confederate treasury would have been much richer than that of the United States."

Not only could the forces of the Confederacy have been completely armed and equipped, but the men could have been well fed, well paid, and the sick and wounded properly cared for. The Government, however, rejected this means of filling the treasury, and limited its financial efforts to printing banknotes, which soon became practically worthless. During the last year of the war the monthly pay of a soldier would scarcely buy one meal for his family. Many men, thus compelled to choose between their loyalty to the State and their duties to their wives and children, left the army, or took every means to avoid military service, in order to support their families.

The proposition, that the Confederate Government should acquire all the cotton in the South, and ship it to Europe to be sold, was made when the problem of financing the war was seriously discussed at the outbreak of hostilities. The owners were ready to accept any fair terms that might be offered; and at that time, as above stated, there would have been no difficulty in putting the plan into operation. But this wise policy was rejected by Mr. Davis and his advisers, in the expectation that the distress caused by the lack of cotton in England and France would lead these two Powers to intervene, and force the United States to raise the blockade. Instead of relying on their own ample resources to win their independence, the Confederate States thus threw away their only means of financing the war. It was one of the worst political blunders in history, and it resulted in the loss of the struggle. With a full treasury, the success of the Confederacy would probably have been assured.

33. Charles W. Ramsdell: THE FINANCIAL BREAKDOWN *

If I were asked what was the greatest single weakness of the Confederacy, I should say, without much hesitation, that it was in this matter of finances. The resort to irredeemable paper money and to excessive issues of such currency was fatal, for it weakened not only the purchasing power of the government but also destroyed economic security among the people. In fact, there seems to be nothing vital that escaped its baneful influence. But if you then ask me how, under the conditions which had existed in April, 1861, the Confederate government could have avoided this pitfall, I can only reply that I do not know. With the small amount of gold and silver coin available in the South and with the initial necessity of using a large portion of that supply in making necessary foreign purchases, how was it possible for this debtor section to accumulate a supply of gold large enough for its needs, or to keep treasury notes at par? The United States government, with infinitely greater financial resources, could not do it! Of course, some contemporary critics of Memminger, the unhappy Confederate Secretary of the Treasury, asserted that the government should have bought up or seized all the cotton, placed it in warehouses, and used it as a basis of credit abroad for the purchase of a navy with which to break up Lincoln's blockade, and thereby open the way for southern exports to go out and for gold and supplies to flow in. Others insisted that the Confederate government should have based its note issues on a straight cotton loan, or that it should have taken over the crop of cotton and other exportable products, paying the planters for all these things with the treasury notes and then made the cotton, tobacco, and other crops, in the absence of gold, the foundation or backing for its currency. But a brief analysis of these proposals will show that they were impracticable. In the first place, at that early stage of the war an attempt of the government to seize the cotton would have been regarded as a flagrant usurpation of unconstitutional authority. To seek to buy it all in the

* Charles W. Ramsdell, *Behind the Lines in the Southern Confederacy* (Baton Rouge: Louisiana State University Press, 1944), pp. 85-89. Reprinted by permission.

open market would have resulted in a great inflation of the price. But if this could have been done, how was the government to get the cotton to Europe when there were no vessels in southern ports to carry it through the blockade? And if a large European loan could have been negotiated on the basis of the cotton, whether exported or held within the country, how could the Confederate government, in the face of the threatening attitude of the United States, have prevailed upon Great Britain or France to sell armed and manned warships to the unrecognized Confederacy? The proponents of the plan airily dismissed all these questions, but the difficulties were real for those who had the responsibility for adopting a definite policy. As to basing the currency upon cotton purchased from the planters, would that have left the government, hard pressed as it was for cash for military expenditures, a sufficient supply of sound money in the treasury? With the cotton locked up within the country and virtually unsalable, would not the treasury have been obliged to issue more currency? Could it have brought the original issue back into its vaults by an initial system of high taxes? No other modern nation has been able to finance successfully a long war by taxation alone. There is no need to go further, for if the issue of an unsupported currency could not be avoided in the beginning there was no place where it could be stopped later. Depreciation and enhancing costs called for more treasury notes which resulted in further depreciation and higher prices; and thus the vicious downward spiral, once entered upon, could not be stopped until utter ruin had resulted. The one point that is insisted upon is that, under the conditions existing at the beginning, the resort to paper currency was unavoidable. And there was no turning back when once that course was taken.

It is very unlikely that the early rise of the price level was caused wholly by the currency policy, for the rise was very uneven and actual physical scarcity accounted for the rapid increase in the cost of such articles as salt, coffee, wool, leather, tea, and medicines. The first efforts to check the rising costs, through embargoes, seizures, and acts prohibiting monopolies and speculation, failed, as they were doubtless bound to fail. They caused hoarding and greater scarcity. The only final remedy was increased production or the use of suitable substitutes. In the winter of 1861-1862, by general popular agreement, a program for a greater production of foodstuffs was undertaken. It worked well enough to have some effect, and before the end of another year popular clamor caused several state governments to enforce the plan by imposing restrictions upon the planting of cotton. During 1863 every state except Louisiana and Texas—in which no such necessity existed—laid restrictions upon the planting of cotton or tobacco. It worked imperfectly, for we find complaints in some districts that many persons were disregarding the law and we hear practically nothing of the enforcement of penalties against them. On the other hand, the astonishing decline in the production of cotton—from 4,500,000 bales in 1861 to less than 300,000 bales in 1864—indicates that there could have been no general disregard of the law with respect to that staple. We have no statistics on the production of tobacco, but there is ample evidence that this crop also was reduced heavily. Although there were failures in both corn and wheat crops in 1862, the yield of 1863, except in the mountain sections and in the areas overrun by the Federals, seems to have been a large one. Especially in those plantation sections far enough in the interior to be safe from Federal attack and where slave labor was still undisturbed, the grain crops were larger than ever before. Again there are no reliable statistics, but if we may accept the statements of many observers, enough grain was raised, especially corn, to feed all the armies, the people, and the livestock. The difficulty was in making an equitable distribution of the grain.

Working out a system of equitable distribution required disentangling a network of interrelated problems. To what extent, in law or equity, were those who had plenty responsible for those who had little or nothing? If it be granted that, in the interests of both humanity and sound public policy, they must accept responsibility, how was the distribution of relief to be administered? Should foodstuffs and other commodities for the suffering be purchased in the open market at exorbitant prices or should they be impressed? Should the local political units be responsible for the relief of their own poor or should the state as a whole assume the obligation? How was prompt transportation of bulky commodities to be obtained over the weak and overloaded railroads and in rural communities where wagons and teams had become so scarce that they hired at $30 or more per day? . . .

34. Richard N. Current: FISCAL POLICIES IMPAIRED THE MORALE OF THE CONFEDERACY *

Certainly, Confederate financing was much less sound and less successful than Union financing. Of the Confederacy's income, to October 1864, almost 60% was derived from the issue of paper money, about 30% from the sale of bonds, and less than 5% from taxation (the remaining 5% arising from miscellaneous sources). Of the Union's income, by contrast, 13% was raised by paper money, 62% by bonds, and 21% by taxes (besides 4% by other means). Thus the Confederacy relied much more upon government notes and much less upon taxation and borrowing than the Union did. Exactly how much paper money was afloat in the wartime South, nobody knows for sure. "Even if we knew the successive amounts of Confederate treasury notes in the hands of the public during the war," John C. Schwab remarks, "this would signify little, as they formed but a part of the currency; the State, municipal, bank, corporate, and individual notes formed the other, and . . . no inconsiderable part." A present-day economist estimates that the stock of money in the South increased approximately eleven fold in the three years from January 1861 to January 1864. In any case, the prices of gold and other commodities were multiplied by much more than eleven. The price of gold, in Confederate dollars, rose eventually to sixty-one (in United States greenbacks it never rose even as high as three). The general price level, in Confederate dollars, soared to ninety or a hundred times

* Richard N. Current, *Why the North Won the Civil War: Economic Considerations* (Nov. 17, 1958, Gettysburg College) (Baton Rouge: Louisiana State University Press, 1964)

its original level. The Confederacy suffered the worst inflation that Americans had known since the Revolutionary War.

In its effort to escape the evils of inflation the Confederate government but compounded them. The Funding Act of 1864, designed to force the exchange of treasury notes for bonds by threatening a partial repudiation of the notes, only speeded the loss in value of the currency. The impressment of government supplies, at less than the inflated market price, caused suppliers to withhold their goods and thus lessened the available amount. Unwittingly, the government defeated its own purposes. "The army suffered from want of food, though in the country at large there was no serious lack of it."

To the later critics of the Davis government it was perfectly obvious that the government should have taxed and taxed and borrowed and borrowed, rather than relying so heavily on the printing of batch after batch of treasury notes. These critics blamed Secretary Memminger, and some historians still blame him (Owsley refers to him as the "measly" Memminger). In truth, however, Memminger was just as well aware of the dangers of inflation as any of his denouncers. They were to have hindsight; he had foresight. But there was little he could do, especially since he possessed neither the force nor the winsomeness of personality to carry the Congress with him. As for taxes, he was all for them, but at the start of the war he had no going machinery of tax collection to work with, and he was dealing with people who had even more than the typical American's resistance to taxation. Besides, cash was comparatively scarce in the Confederacy. The Secretary and the Congress had little choice but to resort to the 1861 requisition upon the states, which the states raised almost entirely by borrowing instead of taxing. As for issuing bonds to sop up the excess currency, Memminger favored that too, but the plain fact was that the people would not or could not buy the bonds in sufficient quantities. Hence his recommendation of the funding scheme to force the sale of bonds—a scheme that Congress carried even farther than he had intended.

There can be no doubt that the government's fiscal policies failed in their main object, namely, to transfer goods efficiently from private to public hands. There is considerable doubt, however, whether Davis or Memminger or any individual was to blame. There also is doubt whether the paper money issues, alone, accounted for the extent of inflation in the South. Actually, the price rise was uneven, and the prices that rose the most were those of goods in short supply, such as leather, wool, coffee, salt, tea, and drugs. So the actual scarcity of some items, as well as the overabundance of money, seems to have been responsible for soaring prices. Moreover, the flight from the currency, at least during the last couple of years of the war, must have been due in part to a growing popular skepticism as to the chances of the Confederacy's ever winning the war and making good on its promises to pay. . . .

Economic conditions gave rise to psychological influences which fatally affected military events. As General Johnston rightly observed, "after the Confederate currency had become almost worthless" the married soldiers from the farms "had to choose between their military service and the strongest obligations they knew—their duties to wives and children." The dilemma of these soldiers was made especially poignant by the actions of Confederate impressment officials. Those officials, as Johnston said, frequently preyed upon the most defenseless of the citizens, especially upon farm women whose husbands were away, in the army. Hard beset by inflation and impressment, wives summoned their soldier husbands home, and, faced with a torturing choice of loyalties, the soldiers often placed family above country. In other ways, too, the fiscal policies of the Confederacy no doubt impaired the morale of both soldiers and civilians. Amid the wild inflation some people grew rich overnight, at least on paper, and other people lost their fortunes just as suddenly. A gambling spirit infected the land, and almost everybody became a speculator of some kind. Those gamblers who lost—and practically all of them lost in the end—naturally were prone to feelings of bitterness and envy. And they directed these feelings against one another as well as against the Yankee foe.

Part XIII

SLAVERY

35. Albert Bushnell Hart: SLAVERY AT THE HEART OF CONFEDERATE FAILURE *

From the moment the first shot was fired on Fort Sumter, to the surrender of the last command in 1865, that slavery for which the South was half-unconsciously fighting was itself undermining and destroying the Confederacy. There were many points of difference between the North and South, there were many mutual accusations of aggression and of bad faith. They all, however, came down to the simple undeniable truth that the North was opposed to slavery and meant to put an end to it, wherever it could be reached; that the South accepted slavery as an inevitable institution, and would permit no interference, direct or indirect. . . . When the war was once begun, the Northern people realized, not that slavery could be destroyed by war, but that the war could be ended by destroying slavery. From the time of the President's preliminary proclamation in September, 1862, it was evident that slavery could be retained only by the success of the South. For slavery as well as independence, the South was fighting; and slavery weakened every blow that was struck and every arm that struck a blow. . . . The slaves proved in other ways a distinct source of weakness: wherever it was possible, and sometimes in circumstances of great difficulty, they gave information to the Union troops; they were our friends, and almost our only friends, in a region of the enemy. And although the slaves refused to rise, they had no conscientious scruples against running away. . . . Of these black refugees there were enlisted as soldiers no less than 186,097 troops. They replaced Northern troops

* Albert Bushnell Hart, "Why the South Was Defeated in the Civil War," *Practical Essays on American Government* (New York, 1893), pp. 293-298.

in garrison duty, they fought beside them in the field, and when the United States Government hesitated to squeeze out of reluctant States the additional number of men necessary for the reinforcement of its armies, those men were found among the slaves of the Southern planters.

In still another sense slavery was the cause of the military defeat of the South. We have already seen that the population of the North had received large accessions through immigration. Those accessions were denied to the South chiefly because of slavery. The total number of foreigners found in the eleven seceding States in 1860 was about 233,000, of whom one-fourth were in New Orleans. The man who crossed the ocean to find more favorable conditions of life was not likely to choose a settlement in a part of the country in which labor was considered the mark of an inferior. Still more were the material wealth and military resources of the South diminished by slavery. The land was not less fertile, but, as we have seen, while the population of the slave States in 1869 was two-thirds that of the other States, their land was worth but one-third as much as that of the free States; and the methods of agriculture which impoverished the Southern lands and prevented their development grew out of slavery. The staple cotton crop was not cultivated merely because it was easily sold. It was cultivated because it was profitable to raise it by large gangs of ignorant men. Manufactures were ignored, not because Southerners did not appreciate their importance, but because it was impossible to carry them on efficiently or profitably with slave labor. The imports of the country were small, not merely because it was poor, but because so large a portion of the population was legally disqualified from buying anything for itself. The accumulations of capital were small because the system of slave labor failed to encourage the savings and the investments which made the wealth of the North. The inefficient management of the financial affairs of the Confederacy was due in great part to the want of training in business habits, a result of the primitive methods of agriculture and of transit. The inability to keep up the railroads and to deal with sudden emergencies in time of war, the inferiority in bridge-building and in ship-

building—all these were due, in great part, to the fact
that the South had for more than three-quarters of a
century deliberately chosen a system of slavery, while
the neighboring States had deliberately chosen a system
of freedom. . . .

The great and fundamental difference between the
sections was that in one of them the presence of a dependent race, and still more the existence of human
slavery, had affected the social and the economic life of
the people; that the productive energies of the North
were employed while those of the South were dormant.
The iron, the coal, the lumber, and the grain of the
North were drawn out by the intelligent combination of
the labor of the whole people; while in the South they
remained undeveloped because it seemed to the commercial interest of the large landowners to perpetuate a
system of agriculture founded on African slavery. For
this mistake, for this preference for a system which had
been abandoned by all other nations of the Teutonic
race, the South paid a fearful penalty in the Civil War.
Slavery had enfeebled the defenders of slavery, and they
and the institution which they strove to protect fell together.

36. Allan Nevins: THE SOUTHERN DILEMMA*

Yet it would be unjust to lay the main responsibility
for a want of passion and inspiration upon the deficiencies of Davis and his colleagues. The final reason why
this Administration exhibited so little of these qualities
lies deeper than any personal limitations.

The South faced two great dilemmas. One, which has
been treated so fully by historians that it is unnecessary
to dwell upon it, was the practical political choice between State Rights and far-reaching drastic measures for
the survival of the Confederacy. . . .

The other and greater Southern dilemma was moral
in character; and in it lies the principal reason why the

* Reprinted with permission of the publisher from *The States-
    manship of the Civil War*, pp. 50-56, by Allan Nevins.
    Copyright 1953 by The Macmillan Company.

Jefferson Davis Adminstration could never display the passion—the moral earnestness—which we find in Washington and Bolivar, Mazzini and Masaryk. The Confederacy emerged as a paladin of the ideas of freedom and self-determination. It also emerged as a great slaveholding nation; in Buchanan's words, the one important government in Christendom which had not abolished or was not in progress to abolish slavery. On the one side, it fought for a noble ideal of liberty; on the other, for the institution of servitude. It stood in an equivocal position on the world stage. Gladstone said: "There is no war except one, the war for liberty, that does not contain in it elements of corruption as well as of misery."

A thoughtful Southerner, Nathaniel W. Stephenson, wrote some years ago that the South had hopelessly compromised itself in not taking action, ten or fifteen years before 1861, to convert slavery into serfdom. Certainly it faced a crippling moral dilemma just after secession. For if it hoped to foster widespread foreign support, or to stimulate its own advanced and idealistic elements to desperate exertions, it must promise a grand amelioration of slavery, while if it made such a promise—as not a few voices even in 1861 demanded—it would hopelessly offend those who, like R. M. T. Hunter, exclaimed: "What did we secede for if not to save our slaves?"

Everyone is familiar with the protestation, "The Confederacy did not fight for slavery"; the argument, "Slavery was the occasion, not the cause, of the war"; and the question, "How could slavery have been the main issue when so heavy a majority of Southerners had no slaves and wanted none?" We all know that Robert E. Lee emancipated his slaves and pronounced slavery a misfortune; that Stonewall Jackson never owned but two slaves and gave both an opportunity to earn their freedom; that Joseph E. Johnston never had a slave and disliked the institution; that Matthew Fontaine Maury termed slavery a curse; and that A. P. Hill never had a slave and thought slavery a deplorable evil.

Unhappily, it is equally true that when the Confederacy was created many Southerners expected to bulwark and extend slavery. In the first Congress some designing men introduced a bill for reviving the slave trade; that is, providing that if a slave ship were "wrecked" on the Southern coast, the Negroes were to be sold at auction. Alexander H. Stephens's famous cornerstone speech was received with acclamation in much of the South, as with hot condemnation in much of the North and of Europe. "Our new government," he said, "is founded upon the opposite idea [to that of the Declaration of Independence]; its foundations are laid, its cornerstone rests, upon the great truth that the Negro is not equal to the white man, that slavery—subordination to the superior race—is his natural and normal condition. . . . This stone which was rejected by the first builders, is become the chief stone of the corner in our new edifice."

The basic attitudes of the South toward slavery of course form much too complex a subject for brief analysis. It would perhaps be roughly fair to say, however, that the more enlightened Southerners were fighting for the right to deal with the joint problems of slavery and race adjustment in their own time and on their own terms. Most informed men realized that slavery was not an institution which would last forever; that soon it would have to be modified, and eventually, relinquished. They knew that the South could not maintain it very long after it ceased to serve a useful economic and social service, and that its utility was nearing an end. They wished, however, to choose the hour and method by which they should decree its gradual extinction. Knowing the complexity of the problem, they did not desire to be whirled into a catastrophic social revolution.

Why, we may ask, did the Confederate leaders not say this? If they announced that the new nation regarded slavery as a transitional system, and would soon study plans for abolishing the internal slave trade, legalizing slave marriages, and providing education for slave children, a host of Europeans might have moved to their side. "See," conservative Britons and Frenchmen might have said, "the Southern republic already goes beyond anything the North has dared to propose." Still more important, an announcement of this policy would have accentuated the Northern divisions. Even as it was, the Copperheads formed a powerful body, and the Laodiceans were numerous. Strengthened by such a pronouncement, the disloyal, the peace-loving, and the faint-hearted might, as Lee continued to win victories, have become irresistible.

But, in the light of thirty years of Southern defensiveness, the obstacles before so bold a step seemed insuperable. An announcement sufficiently strong to impress public opinion abroad and in the North would have shaken the Lower South to its foundations. There came a time when a more reckless, more desperate, or more convinced Confederate Government might really have acted. After Chickamauga in 1863 General Patrick Cleburne, appalled by the depletion of Southern ranks and the difficulty of obtaining recruits for the Western forces, prepared a careful paper advising the emancipation and enlistment of slaves. Letters in the Bragg Collection at the Western Reserve Historical Society show that this paper was signed by Generals Hardee, Polk, Cheatham, Hindman, and others.

Bragg himself referred to it as representing an "abolitionist" movement and as sponsored by the new "Abolition Party of the South." When early in 1864 it found its way by an unfriendly hand to Davis, he wrote that he appreciated the patriotic motive of the fourteen officers who had signed it, but that it was impolitic to make so controversial a document public, and he wished it suppressed. He knew that any decided step in that direction would split the South asunder. At this time even so mild an interference with slavery as the attempt of the Confederate Government to impress 20,000 slaves for labor purposes aroused the bitterest resentment. Governor Vance flatly rejected the national requisition, while South Carolina and Florida passed laws which practically nullified the Confederate statute.

The South was the prisoner of its dilemma. The one course Davis and his associates felt able to take was to remain silent—and silence implied the rejection of a constructive policy. Throughout the war the frozen taciturnity of Davis, Stephens, Benjamin and others on slavery gave Europe and the North no option but to believe that Confederate victory would mean the perpetuation of the institution; nay, would probably mean its extension over adjacent Caribbean areas. The government's blunder in sending Yancey as its envoy to England helped confirm that view, for England knew

Yancey as an arch-defender of slavery and an advocate of reviving the slave trade. John Bright scornfully repeated Stephens's cornerstone declaration in Exeter Hall. Goldwin Smith, the Duke of Argyll, Cairnes, John Stuart Mill and other sympathizers with the North made the most of similar proslavery utterances. As discussion of slavery had been tabu in the South before the war, so now it remained the skeleton locked in the closet.

Between the Scylla of world opinion and the Charybdis of Southern pride, sensitiveness, and economic interest, Confederate statesmanship stood immobile. Eventually it went to shipwreck on both. By the end of 1863 all hope of foreign intervention was gone, and by the beginning of September, 1864, all chance of Democratic victory in the North was ended. Yet the movement for the enlistment (and emancipation) of slaves had, without governmental encouragement, taken on strength. Late in 1864 General Lee was converted to it. Jefferson Davis himself finally came over. In a message of November 7, 1864, he proposed enlisting 40,000 Negroes for service, with a grant of freedom to all willing fighters. He also expressed doubt whether "the private right of property [in human beings] can consistently and beneficially be continued."

But desperate as the Confederate position had then become, the stand of Davis and the still bolder activities of Benjamin provoked a wild storm. When Benjamin at the famous meeting held at the African Church in Richmond on February 9, 1865, proposed a general enlistment of Negro soldiers, with the promise, "You are free," his doctrine was denounced as revolutionary, and Wigfall introduced in Congress a resolution that the country had lost confidence in him.

Years after the war ended Judah P. Benjamin walked home from a Mayfair dinner party with William H. Russell. The journalist reminded the Southern exile that, when Attorney-General in Montgomery, he had predicted that within a year Britain would break the blockade. "When your factories are closed," Benjamin had then said, in effect, "when the Mississippi is floating cotton by thousands of bales, and all our wharves are full, it is inevitable that the Yankees will come to grief in the effort to coerce us." Russell, as the two strolled down

Park Lane, spoke of the failure of the prophecy. "Ah, yes," responded Benjamin. "I was mistaken. I did not believe that your government would allow such misery to be visited on your workers, such loss to be inflicted on your manufacturers. I did not believe the people would have borne it."

The Lancashire operatives had borne it because of the weight of moral imponderables. They would not lend their support to a great slaveholding nation. They had pondered *Uncle Tom's Cabin*. They knew something of the history of the British anti-slavery movement. Their spokesmen in Parliament were Cobden, Bright, and Forster. And although their wives were ragged and their children hungry, they were on the side of human freedom. So it was with certain wavering segments of Northern opinion. Not least among the decisive battles of the war was this struggle for the control of British and Northern opinion, and not the smallest of the Northern victories was that won in the streets of Lancashire and at the Northern polling places.

The Southern republic indeed had the seeds of death implanted in it at birth. But there were two kinds of seeds—State Rights and slavery; and of the two slavery was the more important, for it deprived Southern states-manship of all chance of expressing that passion, that soul-stirring inspiration which alone could make the new nation invincible and raise up friends for it beyond its borders. . . .

Part XIV

THE LOSS OF NERVE

37. Edward A. Pollard: THE DECAY OF PUBLIC SPIRIT *

Most of the wars memorable in history have terminated with some momentous and splendid crisis of arms. Generally some large decisive battle closes the contest; a grand catastrophe mounts the stage; a great scene illuminates the last act of the tragedy. It was not so with the war of the Confederates. And yet there had been every reason to anticipate a dramatic termination of the contest. A war had been fought for four years; its scale of magnitude was unprecedented in modern times; its operations had extended from the silver thread of the Potomac to the black boundaries of the western deserts; its track of blood reached four thousands of miles; the ground of Virginia had been kneaded with human flesh; its monuments of carnage, its spectacles of desolation, its altars of sacrifice stood from the wheat-fields of Pennsylvania to the vales of New Mexico. It is true that the armies of the Confederacy had been dreadfully depleted by desertions; but in the winter of 1864-'5, the belligerent republic had yet more than a hundred thousand men in arms east of the Mississippi River. It was generally supposed in Richmond that if the Confederate cause was ever lost it would be only when this force had been massed, and a decisive field fixed for a grand, multitudinous battle. This idea had run through the whole period of the war; it was impossible in Richmond to imagine the close of the contest without an imposing and splendid catastrophe. In the very commencement of the war, when troops were gaily marching to the first line of battle in Virginia, President Davis had made an address in the camps at Rockett's, declaring that whatever

* Edward A. Pollard, *The Lost Cause* (New York: E. B. Treat, 1866), pp. 726-729.

misfortunes might befall the Confederate arms, they would rally for a final and desperate contest, to pluck victory at last. He said to the famous Hampton Legion: "When the last line of bayonets is levelled, I will be with you."

How far fell the facts below these dramatic anticipations! The contest decisive of the tenure of Richmond and the fate of the Confederacy was scarcely more than what may be termed an "affair," with reference to the extent of its casualties, and at other periods of the war its list of killed and wounded would not have come up to the dignity of a battle in the estimation of the newspapers. Gen. Lee's entire loss in killed and wounded, in the series of engagements that uncovered Richmond and put him on his final retreat, did not exceed two thousand men. The loss of two thousand men decided the fate of the Southern Confederacy! The sequence was surrender from the Potomac to the Rio Grande. The whole fabric of Confederate defence tumbled down at a stroke of arms that did not amount to a battle. There was no last great convulsion, such as usually marks the final struggles of a people's devotion or the expiring hours of their desperation. The word "surrender" travelled from Virginia to Texas. A four years' contest terminated with the smallest incident of bloodshed; it lapsed; it passed by a rapid and easy transition into a profound and abject submission.

There must be some explanation of this flat conclusion of the war. It is easily found. Such a condition could only take place in a thorough demoralization of the armies and people of the Confederacy; there must have been a general decay of public spirit, a general rottenness of public affairs when a great war was thus terminated, and a contest was abandoned so short of positive defeat, and so far from the historical necessity of subjugation.

There has been a very superficial, and, to some people, a very pleasant way of accounting for the downfall of the Southern Confederacy, by simply ascribing it to the great superiority of the North in numbers and resources. This argument has had a great career in the newspapers and in small publications; and the vulgar mind is easily imposed upon by the statistical parallel and the arith-

metical statement, inclined as it is to limit its compre-
hension of great historical problems to mere material
views of the question. We shall give this argument the
benefit of all it contains, and state it in its full force. Thus,
it is correctly said that official reports in Washington
show that there were called into the Federal service from
the Northern States 2,656,553 men during the war, and
that this number is quite one-third as many as all the
white men, women, and children of the Southern States.
Again, the figures in the War Department at Washington
show that on the 1st of May, 1865, the military force
of the North was 1,000,516 men of all arms; while the
paroles taken in the Confederacy officially and conclu-
sively show that the whole number of men within its
limits under arms was exactly 174,223. Thus, it is said,
putting the number 1,000,516 against 174,223, and taking into account the superiority of the North in the war
materiel, there is sufficient reason for the failure of the
Confederate cause without looking for another.

This explanation of failure is of course agreeable to
the Southern people. But the historical judgment rejects
it, discovers the fallacy, and will not refuse to point it
out. It is simply to be observed that the disparity of
military force, as between North and South stated above,
is not the natural one; and that the fact of only 174,223
Confederates being under arms in the last period of the
war was the result of mal-administration, the defective
execution of the conscription law, the decay of the volun-
teer spirit, the unpopularity of the war, and that these
are the causes which lie beyond this arithmetical inequality, which, in fact, produced the greater part of it, and
which must be held responsible in the explanation. The
fallacy consists in taking the very results of Confederate
mal-administration, and putting them in comparison
against a full exhibition of Northern power in the war.

The only just basis of comparison between the military
forces of North and South is to be found in a careful
parallel statement of the populations. This excludes all
question of administration and political skill. Fortunately
we have precise data for the estimate we propose. If
we add to the Free States the four Slave States that followed their lead, under more or less compulsion, Delaware, Maryland, Missouri, and Kentucky, and to these

the districts at Federal command from an early period of the war, say half of Tennessee and Louisiana and a third of Virginia, we have a population, by the census of 1860, of 23,485,722 on the Federal side. This leaves under the rule of the Confederacy 7,662,325. There is no doubt that this superiority of the North in numbers had great weight; that it contributed much to the discomfiture of the Confederacy; that it must be taken largely into any explanation of the results of the war—but the great question, at last, remains, was this numerical inequality, of itself, sufficient to determine the war in favour of the North, considering the great compensation which the South had in superior animation, in the circumstance of fighting on the defensive, and, above all, in the great extent of her territory. We fear that the lessons and examples of history are to the contrary, and we search in vain for one instance where a country of such extent as the Confederacy has been so thoroughly subdued by any amount of military force, *unless where popular demoralization has supervened*. If war was a contest on an open plain, where military forces fight a duel, of course that inferiour in numbers must go under. But war is an intricate game, and there are elements in it far more decisive than that of numbers. At the beginning of the war in America all intelligent men in the world and the Southern leaders themselves knew the disparity of population and consequently of military force as between the North and South; but they did not on that account determine that the defeat of the South was a foregone conclusion, and the argument comes with a bad grace from leaders of the Confederacy to ascribe now its failure to what stared them in the face at the commencement of the contest, and was then so lightly and even insolently dismissed from their calculation. The judgment of men who reflected, was that the South would be ultimately the victor, mainly because it was impossible to conquer *space;* that her subjection was a "geographical impossibility"; that three millions of men could not garrison her territory; that a country so vast and of such peculiar features—not open as the European countries, and traversed everywhere by practicable roads, but wild and difficult with river, mountain, and swamp, equivalent to successive lines of military fortifications,

welted, as it were, with natural mounds and barriers—
could never be brought under subjection to the military
power of the North. And these views were severely just;
they are true forever, now as formerly; but they proceeded on the supposition that the *morale* of the Confederacy would be preserved, and when the hypothesis
fell (mainly through mal-administration in Richmond)
the argument fell with it.

There is but one conclusion that remains for the dis-
passionate student of history. Whatever may be the
partial explanations of the downfall of the Southern
Confederacy, and whatever may be the various excuses
that passion and false pride, and flattery of demagogues,
may offer, the great and melancholy fact remains that
the Confederates, with an abler Government and more
resolute spirit, might have accomplished their independence. . . .

38. Edward Channing: THE LOSS OF NERVE *

In the spring of 1865, the Confederacy collapsed with
a speed and a thoroughness that was entirely unexpected,
except by a few of the leading men on both sides of the
line. Nor is the catastrophe easy to understand or to
describe. In April, 1865, the Confederacy was not beaten
from a military point of view. Lee had thirty thousand
men, more or less, Joseph E. Johnston had as many and,
scattered through Georgia, Alabama, and Mississippi
were other thousands and, west of the Mississippi River,
there were twenty or twenty-five thousand more. All in
all, in the first days of April, when Lee broke away from
Petersburg, there must have been from one hundred and
fifty to two hundred thousand men answerable to the
orders of the Adjutant General at Richmond. Of these,
Lee, on his last return, February 28, 1865, reported
"present for duty," that is with the colors, with arms
in their hands, and ready to step into the fighting line,
fifty-nine thousand out of an "aggregate" of one hundred

* Reprinted with permission of the publisher from *History of
    the United States,* Vol. VI, pp. 612-624, by Edward Chan-
    ning. Copyright 1925 by The Macmillan Company, re-
    newed 1953 by Alice Channing and Elizabeth C. Fuller.

and sixty thousand "present and absent," and Ewell, on March 20 following, reported forty-five hundred for duty and nearly ten thousand "present and absent" in the Department of Richmond. Of course, an army melts away in times of stress and disaster, but the disappearance of the Confederate soldiers from the rolls between December, 1864, and April, 1865, is one of the puzzles of the history of the Confederacy.

The Southern people, had they so wished, could have held out for a long time. The Texans, alone, might have fought on until the Northern people would have become so wearied that they would have preferred to let them go in peace rather than send their sons and brothers to continue useless warfare. With this opinion, Jefferson Davis was in entire agreement. At Greensboro, in April, 1865, while on his way southward from Richmond, he summoned to a conference General Breckinridge, then Secretary of War, and Joseph E. Johnston, the commander of the only considerable Confederate army east of the Mississippi River. He tried to induce them to agree to an opinion that it was possible to continue the war. Johnston absolutely disagreed with him and told him that the people were beaten and knew it. Later, at Abbeville, in South Carolina, on one of the first days of May, Jefferson Davis held his last council of war,—this time, with the commanders of the brigades that still clung to him and with Generals Breckinridge and Bragg. At the beginning of the conference, he was affable, dignified, and the personification of high and undaunted courage. Upon being asked for their opinions, the brigade commanders in turn said that "They and their followers despaired of successfully conducting the war, and doubted the propriety of prolonging it." They would risk battle to secure the safety of Mr. Davis "but would not ask their men to struggle against a fate, which was inevitable, and forfeit all hope of a restoration to their homes and friends." Davis answered that he wished to hear no plan for his safety—"that twenty-five hundred brave men were enough to prolong the war, until the panic had passed away, and they would then be a nucleus for thousands more." There was no reply. He then said, bitterly, that "he saw all hope was gone—that all the friends of the South were prepared to consent to her degradation." When he left the room he faltered and leaned upon General Breckinridge for support. Judging from the history of other wars and other revolutions, the end had not come and was not even in sight had the Southern people, or the mass of the people of the seceded States, wished to continue the fight for Southern independence. . . .

On October 6, 1864, General Gorgas wrote in his "Journal" that the harrowed and overworked soldiers were getting worn out. "They see nothing before them but certain death, and have, I fear, fallen into a sort of hopelessness and are dispirited," the only cure that occurred to Gorgas was to limit the term of service to five years and to employ slaves in every possible capacity, even as guards and soldiers. Meetings were held in North Carolina and Alabama in 1864 and, possibly, in other States at which methods of bringing about peace at once and by State action were discussed; but these movements, whatever they amounted to, came to speedy and untimely ends. It would seem that there was an available military population within the one-time limits of the Confederacy that was amply sufficient to keep up resistance to Northern armies, had there been the enthusiasm for the cause that there was in 1861. It has been usual to attribute the sudden ending of the war to scarcity of arms and munitions and to a lack of food.

Until the end of the year 1863 there is reason to suppose that the Confederate armies relied upon foreign munitions, for use in the field, and it is well known that arms that came through the blockade into Charleston were used by the Confederates in the battle of Chickamauga. . . . On April 8, 1864, General Gorgas wrote in his journal that three years ago today he took charge of the Ordinance Department, and had succeeded beyond his utmost expectations. Large arsenals had been organized; a "superb powder mill" had been built at Augusta, lead smelting works established at Petersburg, and turned over to the Nitre and Mining Bureau, when it was separated from his department at his request. A cannon foundry had been established at Macon, bronze foundries there and at Augusta, besides a manufactory of carbines, and a rifle factory, and two pistol factories "where three years ago we were not making a gun, a pistol, nor

a sabre, no shot nor shell (except at the Tredegar
Works), a pound of powder—we now make all these in
quantities to meet the demands of our large armies";
and General Gorgas felt that his time had not been
passed "in vain." . . .

One is astounded at the ingenuity and mechanical ability displayed by the Southerners in this emergency of
their lives. In the production of munitions and of material they faced the same difficulties that they did in
manufacturing textiles and in every industry, and also
in transportation. There was not an adequate labor supply in the South, although the greater part of the male
white population had been conscripted. Many English
mechanics were imported, but they do not seem to have
liked working in factories in the South. It may have
been on account of the climate, or it may have been the
association with work that went side by side with the
slave system. Also it would seem that the Confederate
government itself was not at all skilful in differentiating
the classes of white working men, and utilizing the several
classes to the utmost, in the factories and on the railroads. Some State governors also tried to force the imported workingmen into the military service! But without much success. If any one has doubts as to the capacity
of the South to continue warfare in April, 1865, so far
as war materials are concerned, he has only to read
Gorgas's accounts to satisfy himself that it was not any
dearth of material that brought about the ending in the
spring of 1865.

One of the favorite modes of accounting for the collapse of the Confederacy has been to depict the starving
condition of the Confederate soldier in April, 1865.
This idea is possibly most graphically expressed in the
sentence: "Those twin monsters, hunger and starvation,
forced our gates." Those who hold to this view, point to
the prices paid for food at Richmond in the winter of
1864-1865. It is true that in February, 1865, potatoes
sold for one hundred dollars a bushel at Richmond, and
flour at eighty-eight dollars a barrel. But eighty-eight dollars in Confederate money at that time was the equivalent
of eight dollars and eighty cents in gold, and indeed the
gold price of flour at Richmond in that winter was less
than it was at New York. Also it is interesting to note

that as late as the spring of 1864 it was possible to buy
brown sugar in Richmond, although the price was six
dollars a pound, and also coffee at eight dollars a pound;
but this price was only somewhere between a quarter and
a half a dollar in specie. The Southern food crops of
1862 had been deficient and there was, no doubt, a
scarcity of food in the spring and summer of 1863 and
Lee's invasion of Pennsylvania was partly in answer to
that need. The crops of 1863 and 1864 were good, and
during those years, until the latter part of 1864, quantities
of bacon were imported through the blockade to make
up for the loss of that which in the old days had been
brought into the Southern country from the Ohio Valley.
There is no question but that the operations of Sherman
from Atlanta to Raleigh had seriously interfered with
the transportation service of the Confederacy so that
although Commissary Northrup reported in February,
1865, that two and a half million rations of meat and
seven hundred thousand rations of bread were on the
way to Richmond, it is extremely probable that not much
of it had reached that place in the first part of February,
for President Davis found it necessary to replace his old
friend Northrup, at the head of the Commissary Bureau,
by General I. M. St. John. That officer at once displayed
the same energy and capacity that he had shown at the
head of the Nitre and Mining Bureau. On April 1, 1865,
his assistant, Lieutenant Colonel Williams, reported that
there were at Richmond three hundred thousand rations
of bread and meat; at Danville, five hundred thousand
rations of bread, and one and a half million rations of
meat; and one million six hundred and eighty thousand
more rations of bread and meat at Lynchburg and at
Greensboro. Also it is worth noting that in October,
1864, the navy had on hand four months rations, including one hundred thousand pounds of coffee and thirty
thousand pounds of sugar and one thousand pounds of
tea. Confirming these statements as to food in North
Carolina and Virginia, it may be noted that General
Joseph E. Johnston stated that in February, 1865, there
were in depots between Danville and Weldon rations for
sixty thousand men for more than four months; and at
Charlotte "what we then regarded as large stores of
sugar, coffee, tea, and brandy." "The Georgia Girl,"

Eliza F. Andrews, in her "War-time Journal," recounts that in February, 1865, she went to a rehearsal near Albany, Georgia, and had "a splendid supper, with ice cream and sherbet and cake made of real white sugar." Soon after, she returned to the parental home in Washington, also in Georgia, and fed hundreds of paroled soldiers streaming westward from Appomattox and later from Raleigh,—and it is marvellous to read of the amount of food that was stored away in her father's house. Finally, Jabez L. M. Curry, one of the most prominent of after-the-war Confederates, states in his book that "at the surrender there was on the line of the railways and rivers, between Jackson, Mississippi, and Montgomery, Alabama, enough corn to supply the demand for breadstuffs for a full twelve-month or more." When Richmond was evacuated by the Confederates, they set fire to storehouses filled with foodstuffs and also with munitions of war; at Farmville, and again at Appomattox Station trainloads of food, which were waiting for the Confederates, were captured by the Union soldiers. There was starvation and suffering in Lee's army from Petersburg to Appomattox Court House, but that was due in no way to a scarcity of food within the Confederacy.

It is abundantly evident to the under-surface seeker that by the summer of 1864, and even more so by December of that year, the will to fight had gone from large sections of the Southern people. . . . On January 18, 1865, and again, on March 9, the Confederate Adjutant-General issued a list of twelve hundred officers whose resignations had been accepted by President Davis. The cause for this utter demoralization, as it was, could be stated by any man according to his own preconceived ideas; but a few things may be set down with a reasonable degree of confidence. By the winter of 1864-1865, the "utter hopelessness of the struggle" was borne in upon the people by the terrible losses of life in the fearful battles in the Wilderness in which attack after attack had been made upon the Union lines. Then the constant infringement on the freedom of movement and of employment seems to have been deeply felt. The Confederate soldier had never had much money to send home to his family, but the amount that his monthly wage, paid in Confederate money, would purchase for his wife and children had so diminished that the most zealous enthusiasm weakened. . . .

By the autumn and winter of 1864-1865, whatever the reason, there can be no question as to the amount of absenteeism and desertion from the army. In September, 1864, President Davis stated that "two-thirds of our men are absent—some sick, some wounded, but most of them absent without leave." At about the same time a committee of the Congress at Richmond reported that while the country "notoriously swarms with skulkers from military service and absentees and deserters from the army" they were asked to provide new soldiers. As the autumn wore on, it became noticeable that the deserters from the Confederate lines from Petersburg brought their arms with them, which they had not done before. In February and March, 1865, the commanders constantly came across "intercepted appeals *from friends at home* to the soldiers to desert." On the 31st of December, 1864, the field return of Hagood's South Carolina Brigade shows that 1,592 were present and 2,016 were absent; of the latter 577 were reported as "missing" and 529 as "absent without leave" and 15 of these were officers. General Hagood noted that the number of this latter group was "ominous of that change in popular sentiment which now began to connive at a dereliction of duty" which earlier had been deemed "little less shameful than desertion." He states that Hardee left Charleston with "upward of 10,000 men" and had four thousand only when he reached the North Carolina border; although there had been no combat on the way, "straggling and desertion had done the work."

Parts of some States of the Confederacy were filled with deserters and with fugitives from conscription. These joined with Unionists and with escaped Union prisoners and held the countryside in terror. In portions of Virginia, in parts of the Carolinas, and in many other bits of the Confederacy, the ordinary bonds binding together society had disappeared. . . .